Sand and Water Play:
Simple, Creative Activities for Young Children

Sherrie West and Amy Cox

Illustrations: K. Whelan Dery

DEDICATION

We dedicate this book to the Melba S. Lehner Children's School at Weber State University for their philosophy to always put the child first.

Sand and Water Play

Simple, Creative Activities for Young Children

Sherrie West
and Amy Cox

gryphon house®, Inc.
Beltsville, MD

Copyright © 2001 Sherrie West and Amy Cox
Published by Gryphon House, Inc.
10726 Tucker Street, Beltsville MD 20705
Visit us on the web at www.gryphonhouse.com

Library of Congress Cataloging-in-Publication Data

West, Sherrie 1957–
    Sand and water play: simple, creative activities for young children / Sherrie West and Amy Cox; illustrations, K. Whelan Dery.
        p. cm.
    Includes index.
    ISBN 0-87659-247-7
    1. Early childhood education—Activity programs—Handbooks, manuals, etc. I. Cox, Amy, 1968– II. Title.

LB1139.35.A37 W427 2001
372.13--dc21

                                                    2001023918

Illustrations: K. Whelan Dery
Cover photograph: Straight Shots Product Photography, Ellicott City, Maryland.

BULK PURCHASE

DISCLAIMER

Table of Contents

PREFACE

INTRODUCTION
How to Use This Book 8

ART ACTIVITIES
Balls and Paint 14
Fingerpainting 16
Shaving Cream 18
Bubble, Bubble, Print 20
Sun Catchers 22

DRAMATIC PLAY ACTIVITIES
Baking 26
Washing Babies 28
Plant Nursery 30
Fossils 32

ENVIRONMENT ACTIVITIES
Construction Workers 36
Astronauts 38
Marine Dock 40
Snow 42
Cars and Airplanes 44
Digging for Dinos 46
Homey Habitats 48

OUTDOORS ACTIVITIES
Backyard Beach Party 52
Sand Castles, Canals, and Tunnels 54
Sand Stew 56
Garden 58
Car Wash 60
Biggie Bubbles 62
Rainbow Maker 64

SCIENCE ACTIVITIES

Air Moves Things 68
Magnets 70
See and Feel 72
Float and Sink 74
Melting Pot 76
Oobleck 78
Vinegar and Baking Soda 80
Ice Cubes 82
Air and Water Wonders 84
Test Tubes 86

WATER ACTIVITIES

Dump and Fill 90
Waterwheels 92
Legos and Water 94
Tongs and Balls 96
Boats 98
Pipes and Accordian Tubing 100

MISCELLANEOUS ACTIVITIES

Putty or Dough 104
Pumpkins 106
Wild and Wacky Word Strips 108
Crazy Counting 110

CHARTS

Prediction Chart 114
Tally Sheet 115
Color Mixing 116
Signs 117

RECIPES

Homemade Silly Putty 120
Playdough 120
Frilly Bubbles 121
Print Maker Bubbles 121
Hardy Bubbles 121
Brewing Bubbles 122
Oobleck 122
Salt Paint 122
Soap Paint 123
Sand Paint 123

INDEX 125

Preface

There is a growing emphasis on learning basic skills and concepts at a young age. Because children learn best when they can control and act upon their own environment, we firmly believe that they need many opportunities to play with different mediums, such as sand, water, clay, playdough, and so on. Creative play and hands-on experiences are essential to the development of well-balanced children. Children need to have the opportunity to see, touch, learn, and express themselves. Therefore, teachers have the responsibility to create an environment that can stimulate children's senses and curiosity.

Teachers may not be aware of the importance of a sand and water table and how it can increase learning in a school setting. Every child, including one who is developmentally delayed, can benefit from using the sand and water table. Experiences in the sand and water table have a sensory motor quality, which is a unique attribute that allows children to release tension in a non-threatening environment and help them develop new skills, increasing their confidence. Sand and water experiences will also help children grow in all areas of development. For example, some children will have their first positive social interactions at the sand and water table. Also, a child may be more comfortable trying a writing experience at the sand and water table. That child may then use this new-found confidence to try a literacy activity elsewhere in the classroom. Perhaps he or she can have a positive experience with letters and be more willing to try different activities. In addition, a child can be motivated to increase and use his or her verbal skills in this setting. Sand and water activities allow children to have hands-on experiences, gain confidence, and move to higher levels of learning. These few examples demonstrate the importance of using a sand and water table in the classroom every single day. To help teachers accomplish this goal, this book provides a collection of activities written by teachers who work in an early childhood university lab setting.

Introduction

We have created the activities in this book to enhance the development—intellectual, literacy, emotional, social, physical, and diversity—of the whole child. The activities are geared for children ages three to six years old.

We believe that looking at the individual child and recognizing his or her specific needs is critical. It is important that teachers choose an activity based on a child's needs and interests. First, observe the child to determine what is most important for him or her to learn. Then, choose the activity according to the child's development and what that child is capable of learning. You might want to choose an activity because of a specific child's strength or weakness. Plan and prepare the activity, adapting the level of difficulty depending upon the children's grade level. Most of the activities are written for the preschool setting. However, there are variations and ideas in the activities that you can use in kindergarten or first grade to teach reading, math, and other areas of development. Always remember that the best activities are open-ended and hands-on. Be creative and adapt the activity to meet children's needs. Remember, it is not the product that matters most, but the process.

An important aspect of using the sand and water table is to keep it safe and healthy for children. The following are some guidelines to follow:

1. Teachers should never leave children unattended around any type of water, indoors or out. An adult must be present at all times.
2. Empty the sand and water table each day to prevent germs from growing.
3. Sanitize the tub and supplies after each use.
4. Make sure the children wash their hands before and after using the sand and water table.
5. Color the water with washable paint or liquid watercolors.
6. Make sure the water level in the sand and water table is age-appropriate. For example, when planning for toddlers, fill it about 2" (5 cm) deep. For three- and four-year-olds, fill it approximately 5" (12 cm) deep.

HOW TO USE THIS BOOK

Objectives

Objectives can be long-term goals or short-term goals. Short-term goals, which are generated from long-term goals, give direction to daily teaching. They should be specific for the individuals in your class. The objectives we created for each activity in this book are goals we believe can be met through that specific activity (short-term goals). When doing an activity, you can focus on one, two, or more of the suggested objectives. However, if none of the suggested objectives will work for you, change them to fit the children's needs.

As you incorporate our objectives into your lesson plans, make sure they are measurable and can be met. The only way a teacher knows whether or not an objective has been met or a child has learned something is through evaluating and comparing what the child already knew with what the child now knows. The teacher knows if the activity is effective if he or she can see a changed outcome in the child's behavior through observation. Evaluation is critical. A teacher must know if his or her activities are helping the child progress through the developmental sequence. If the desired objective is not met and does not enhance the child's development, the teacher must reassess the child's needs and make new short-term goals.

If you do not meet your long-term goals, then develop more short-term goals or consider the possibility that what you want the children to learn is not appropriate for their developmental sequence. Becoming familiar with developmentally appropriate practices will help you make informed decisions while planning.

The purpose of early education is to foster competency in young children in all areas of development. The teacher will develop curriculum through activities based on objectives that allow total learning to occur. It is possible to develop the children's emotional, social, physical, and cognitive skills. It could appear overwhelming, but as you break it down into smaller components, the parts will unfold. You will see that it is possible to enhance the whole child.

Intellectual—Objectives where children can increase their factual information and develop problem-solving skills by applying acquired knowledge, facts, and techniques in their world. Child will learn to group and classify, arrange things in logical order, identify and match, and understand cause-and-effect. They will gain an understanding of the scientific method as they observe, predict, try out solutions, observe the results, and evaluate information that will help them to identify numbers, count, and understand one-to-one correspondence. They also gain an understanding of conservation as they experiment with measuring.

Literacy—Objectives where children are exposed to written and verbal communication. Children will express themselves verbally and increase their communication skills by listening to others and understanding what they say. They will learn to carry on a conversation by taking turns and listening to others. Teachers will ask open-ended questions so the children can develop thinking skills. The children's ability to follow directions will be enhanced. They will be exposed to print and will understand that letter symbols create words. They will gain an awareness that spoken words can be written down.

Emotional—Objectives where children gain self-esteem and develop independence. Through meeting emotional objectives, children will release tension, concentrate for longer periods of time, become absorbed in an activity, and channel their behavior in appropriate ways. The children will understand a range of feelings, both negative and positive, and will be encouraged to recognize these feelings and express them in appropriate ways. Children will empathize with their peers and understand that others can be hurt. They will have the opportunity to express their own ideas and gain an appreciation of others' ideas and feelings. Children are naturally drawn to the sand and water table because of its sensorimotor quality, allowing them to separate from their parents more easily. The sand and water table also allows children to release and get rid of their frustrations through sensorimotor play.

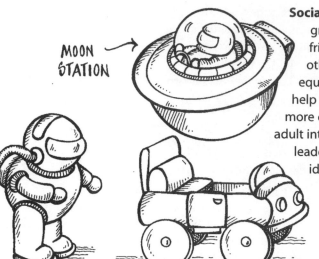

MOON STATION →

Social—Objectives where children can work together as a group and negotiate with others. Children will develop friendly, close relationships. They learn to listen to each other and work out differences. Children will learn to share equipment. Children will be encouraged and expected to help each other as they learn together. Children can become more competent to work out their own problems without adult intervention. As children play with each other, they accept leadership responsibility and allow others to contribute their ideas to the play situation. Children will have opportunities to become involved in imaginative play, and they will incorporate what they know as they play. Through play, they will make sense of their world.

Physical—Objectives where children can develop eye-hand coordination and increase their fine motor skills. Eye-hand coordination includes stringing beads, stacking, pouring, spooning, scooping, snapping, and putting together manipulative materials. Children will increase their fine motor skills as they practice cutting and writing. Children will compare textures such as hard, smooth, runny, and soft as they become involved in hands-on activities. Children will develop awareness of their body space as they respect each other's personal physical space.

Diversity—Objectives where children are allowed opportunities to recognize and accept each others' similarities and differences in a non-judgmental way. Children will capitalize on similarities in the world around them. Children will be encouraged to experience non-traditional roles of men and women. They will gain an understanding of different occupations and families. They will become more aware of similarities in gender roles, race, special needs, and culture. Activities will encourage intergroup mixing when two or more languages and cultures are shared in the classroom. They will learn to communicate and respect each other as they play together.

SUGGESTED MATERIALS

As you view the list of materials needed in each activity, be resourceful. It can take several years to gather all the materials needed for these activities. Modify and start out simply. Ask businesses and parents to donate materials to help cut the cost of your supplies. Hunt for bargains in dime and dollar stores. The following is a list of ideas for mediums (other than sand or water) and supplies to use with the mediums in the sand and water table. The activities in this book use a combination of these mediums and supplies. As with any classroom material, supervise the use of mediums and supplies, especially if there are children in your class who put things into their mouths.

The authors do not encourage teachers to use food, such as rice, oatmeal, pasta, beans, and so on for sensorimotor activities. Some early childhood educators find these materials valuable for providing soothing experiences for emotionally troubled children. However, to make it clear to children that food is for eating, not playing, and to be sensitive to the issue of hunger, we suggest limiting sensory materials to the use of other non-edible materials listed on the following page.

Mediums	Supplies	
aquarium rocks	animal figures	muffin tins
beads/lacing	balance scales	people figures
bird seed	boats	Ping-Pong balls
bubbles	bowls	plastic eggs
cottonseed	buckets	plastic insects
Easter grass	cookie cutters	plastic letters
fingerpaint	dinosaurs	plastic plants
ice cubes	dolls	plastic test tubes
large buttons	egg beaters	scoops
leaves	eyedroppers	shapes
mud and worms	flour sifters	small cars/trucks
nuts and bolts	funnels	small shovels
Oobleck	garlic presses	spinning tops
packing materials	Legos	sponges
playdough	magnifying glasses	strainers
potting soil	marble tunnel	tall containers
rock salt	marbles	tongs and balls
sand (damp)	measuring cups	tubes
sawdust	measuring spoons	water mills
scissors/paper	melon scoops	whisks
shaving cream		
shredded paper		
silly putty		
snow		
soybeans		
straws		
water		

SETTING UP THE ACTIVITY

For some activities, such as Construction Workers (page 36), it is only necessary to set out the materials. Others, though, such as Air and Water Wonders (page 84) require you to follow detailed directions. When specific instructions are necessary, we provide the instructions to accomplish the teacher's goals and objectives. At other times, we provide broad, simple guidelines for setting up the activity.

OPEN-ENDED QUESTIONS

These are questions that teachers can use to help children think and discover on their own. Because questioning is one of the most important skills a teacher can use to stimulate learning, we have included an extended list of open-ended questions below.

> Can you explain what is happening?
> Can you identify them into different parts?
> Can you list three things that happened?
> Can you recall…?
> Can you think of another way?
> Could you improve _____?
> Could you put them into groups?
> How could you change what happened?

How could you determine…?

How could you organize _____ to show _____?

How did _____ happen?

How does this work?

How is…?

How is it related to …?

How would you describe…?

How would you explain…?

How would you solve _____ with what you have learned?

In your own words describe _____.

Suppose you could _____, what could you do?

What can you say about _____?

What choices could you make?

What do you suppose we learned?

What evidence can you find?

What is…?

What is your main idea?

What other way would you do it?

What would happen if …?

What would you do differently?

When did _____ happen?

When did…?

Where is…?

Why did…?

Why did you choose that?

Why do you think…?

Would it be better if…?

SPOTLIGHT WORDS

These are vocabulary words on which to focus during the activity. Teachers should use these words in their verbal communication with the children to help them understand their meaning. You can also write down these words so the children can be exposed to written print on a daily basis.

TIPS

This is information that we have discovered through experience that will enhance sand and water table activities.

Art Activities

Balls and Paint 14

Fingerpainting 16

Shaving Cream 18

Bubble, Bubble, Print 20

Sun Catchers 22

Balls and Paint

OBJECTIVES

Intellectual | Children will gain a better understanding of the components of art, such as line, design, creativity, and form.

Emotional | Children will have a positive outlet for their emotions.

Physical | Children will increase their eye-hand coordination skills.

MATERIALS

Paint smocks

Butcher paper

Tempera paint

Water

Container

Variety of balls, such as bouncy balls, Ping-Pong balls, golf balls, magnetic balls, small plastic balls with holes in them, and so on

White construction paper

SETTING UP THE ACTIVITY

1. Make sure the children wear paint smocks for this activity.
2. Line the sand and water table with butcher paper.
3. Put tempera paint in a container. Thin it with water.
4. Place the balls into the paint.
5. Encourage the children to roll and bounce the paint-covered balls back and forth to each other on top of the paper in the sand and water table.
6. When a child is ready to make a print, place a sheet of white construction paper on top of the design made by the balls, press down, and carefully lift it. Ask the child, "What does it look like?"

Open-Ended Questions
What are other things you can do with the balls?

What did you create? Tell me about it.

Spotlight Words
Aim
Bounce
Catch
Design
Follow
Form
Line
Roll
Shape
Watch

Fingerpainting

OBJECTIVES

Intellectual | Children will learn how to mix together different colors.

Children will learn how to make prints.

Emotional | Children will have their own ideas and put them into action.

Physical | Children will strengthen their small motor muscles.

MATERIALS

Paint smocks

Fingerpaint

White construction paper

Butcher paper

Tablespoon

Liquid starch

Chalk

Large saltshakers

Powdered tempera paint

SETTING UP THE ACTIVITY

1. Make sure the children wear paint smocks for this activity.

2. With each of the following fingerpaint explorations, you can make individual prints of the children's work. In addition, when finished, you can use the painted butcher paper for a class mural to hang in your room.

Fingerpaint—Place small dabs of fingerpaint in the bottom of the sand and water table. Encourage the children to create pictures using their fingers. After the child has made her design, place a piece of white construction paper on top of the design, press down gently, and carefully lift the paper.

Liquid Starch and Chalk—Line the sand and water table with butcher paper. For each child, pour about 1 tablespoon (15 ml) of liquid starch on the paper. Then, encourage the children to dip chalk into the liquid starch and make designs. The starch will carry the colors and make them more vibrant.

PRINT LIFTED OFF BOTTOM OF SAND/WATER TABLE

LIQUID STARCH

SALT SHAKER

POWDERED TEMPERA PAINT

DABS OF FINGER PAINT

Liquid Starch and Powdered Tempera Paint—Line the sand and water table with butcher paper. For each child, pour about 3 to 4 tablespoons (45 to 60 ml) of liquid starch on the paper. Pour powdered tempera paint into large saltshakers. Ask the children to sprinkle powdered tempera paint over the starch. Encourage the children to mix the colors and create pictures.

Open-Ended Questions

What colors do you think look good together?

Spotlight Words

Blend
Colors
Combine
Hue
Merge
Mix
Print
Vibrant

Shaving Cream

OBJECTIVES

Intellectual | Children will experiment with colors and how they mix together.

Literacy | Children will begin to write using alphabet forms.

Emotional | Children will release tension in positive ways.
Children will have their own ideas about how to use materials and will put their ideas into action.

MATERIALS

Paint smocks

Shaving cream*

Liquid washable paint

ABC chart

Objects (see list of supplies on page 11)

SETTING UP THE ACTIVITY

1. Make sure the children wear paint smocks for this activity.
2. It doesn't take a lot of shaving cream to make this activity successful. You will need just enough shaving cream to cover the bottom of the sand and water table.

   Mixing Colors—Put shaving cream into the bottom of the sand and water table and place small drops of liquid washable paint in it. (The primary colors are the best to use.) Then, encourage the children to mix together the colors.

   ABC's—Put shaving cream into the sand and water table. Provide an ABC chart for the children to look at if they need to. Encourage the children to use their fingers to write letters in the shaving cream on the bottom of the sand and water table.

   Creativity—Put shaving cream and other objects in which the children are interested into the sand and water table.

   Note: An adult must supervise this activity at all times to be sure children do not put their shaving cream-covered fingers into their mouths or eyes.

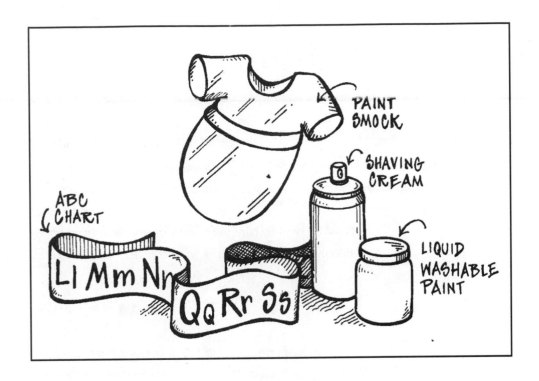

Open-Ended
Questions

What does the shaving
cream feel like?

What colors can you
create?

What does shaving
cream smell like?

Spotlight Words

Colors
Dissolve
Feel
Silky
Smell
Soft

Note: Be sure to limit
both the number of
times and the amount
of time that children
play with shaving
cream. Shaving cream
can cause skin
irritations.

Bubble, Bubble, Print

OBJECTIVES

Intellectual | *Children will learn the beginning schemes or knowledge of science.*

Emotional | *Children will separate from their parents and become involved with a planned activity.*

Children will feel confident and show pride in their work.

Children will approach a task with expectations of success.

MATERIALS

Tall container

Ingredients for bubble recipes (see pages 121-122)

Straws or small tubing (When using straws or small tubing, make sure the children do not share. Each child should have her own straw to ensure that it is sanitary.)

Washable paint

Pie tins

White construction paper

Bubble-making materials (such as bubble wands, heavy raspberry baskets, twisted coat hangers, kitchen utensils, plastic six-pack wings, pipe cleaners twisted into different shapes, and so on)

SETTING UP THE ACTIVITY

1. Try one or more of the following possibilities.

   Straw Blowing—Make Frilly Bubble Solution using the recipe on page 121. Fill tall containers half full with bubble solution, one for each child. Provide each child with straws or small tubing. Encourage the children to fill the sand and water table with the bubbles they blow.

   Bubble Prints—Use the Print Maker Bubbles recipe (page 121) to make bubble solution. Separate the bubble solution into three or four equal parts and add paint to each one to make different colors. Pour each color into separate pie tins and place them in the bottom of the sand and water table. Encourage the children to blow bubbles through their straws, until the bubbles are above the top of the pie tin. Place a piece of white

RECIPE

BLUE PAINT

YELLOW PAINT

RED PAINT

STRAW

WHITE PAPER

PIE TIN WITH BUBBLES

construction paper on top of the pie tin and lift off. This should make a print of the bubbles.

Bubble wands—Use the Brewing Bubbles recipe (page 122) to make bubble solution. Pour the bubble solution into the bottom of the sand and water table, about 2" to 3" (5 cm to 7 cm) full. Add bubble-making materials. Encourage the children to blow away and experiment with all of the different kinds of bubbles they can make.

Use the Brewing Bubbles recipe (page 122)

Tips
Help the children practice blowing through a straw into water before introducing them to the bubble mixture.

Open-Ended Questions
Why do you think some bubbles are small and other bubbles are large?

How long can a bubble last before it pops?

Where do you suppose that bubble went after it popped?

Spotlight Words
Air
Blow
Color
Dark
Large
Light
Medium
Prism
Small
Surface tension
Transparent

Sun Catchers

OBJECTIVES

Emotional | *Children will have a chance to express themselves through creativity.*
Children will experience success by completing a task.
Children will have the opportunity to make their own choices.
Physical | *Children will increase their fine motor skills.*

MATERIALS

Butcher paper
Wax paper
Small pieces of tissue paper, small leaves, flowers, and crayon shavings
Watered-down glue
Iron (teacher only)
Scissors, optional

SETTING UP THE ACTIVITY

1. Line the sand and water table with butcher paper for easy cleanup. Then, place long strips of wax paper on top of the butcher paper.
2. Encourage the children to dip their items (see materials) into the watered-down glue. Then, ask them to place the gluey items on the long sheets of wax paper.
3. Take the wax paper out of the sand and water table and let it dry.
4. Place another piece of wax paper over the design. You or another adult will iron the two sheets together. The children can cut out different shapes or display the whole design in the window. The light will shine through it to make a beautiful sun catcher.

TISSUE PAPER

FLOWERS

BUTCHER PAPER

SMALL LEAVES

CRAYON SHAVINGS

WAX PAPER

WATERED DOWN GLUE

IRON

Tips
Simply let the children create their own designs and enjoy the activity. The children will be influenced by your attitude and judgment about their work. Children are the best judges of their work. They will tell you what it is, and if they think they did a good job or not.

Open-Ended Questions
What can you do with these materials?

What kind of design can you make?

Can you see something in that design?

Spotlight Words
Color
Design
Form
Line
Pattern
Plan
Shape
Style

Dramatic Play Activities

Baking 26

Washing Babies 28

Plant Nursery 30

Fossils 32

Baking

OBJECTIVES

Literacy | Children will begin to understand the relationship between thoughts, spoken words, writing, and reading.

Emotional | Children will respond to questions, discussion, and directions appropriately.

Social | Children will take turns using equipment.

Diversity | Children will accept different gender roles by seeing that it is appropriate for men and women to bake.

MATERIALS

Cooking equipment, such as rolling pins, cookie cutters, cupcake pans, and so on

Mixing bowls and spoons

Measuring cups and spoons

Sifters

Aprons

Playdough

Recipes on cards

Paper and pens

SETTING UP THE ACTIVITY

1. Move the sand and water table to different parts of the room. For example, move it into the Housekeeping area to enrich the children's play.

2. Place cooking materials and equipment in the sand and water table to stimulate children's play. Encourage the children to put on aprons and prepare and "bake" different foods using playdough.

3. Ask the children to bring in their favorite family recipes from home.

4. Also encourage the children to create their own recipes. Ask the children to dictate recipes as you write them down for them. With the children, make a cookbook using real and imaginary recipes. (This makes a great Mother's Day present!)

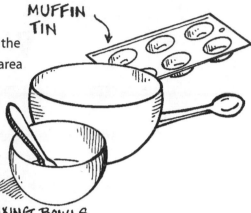

MUFFIN TIN

MIXING BOWLS and SPOONS

A SAMPLE OF A CHILD'S IMAGINARY RECIPE:

Chocolate Cake

2 chocolates

2 eggs

3 cups of sugar

2 cups of pepper

1/2 cup of milk

2 carrots that are cut

That's it!

1. Stir it all for 3 minutes.
2. Turn the oven all the way to 3.
3. Put it in the oven. It needs to cook for 4 minutes.
4. When the oven dings, it is done.
5. Then we can eat it! It makes 11 pieces of cake.

Tips
Remember that children this age are still learning the difference between fantasy and reality.

Open-Ended Questions
What are some things you can make with flour?

What things will you need to make _____?

Spotlight Words
Beat
Blend
Combine
Ingredients
Mix
Recipe
Separate
Stir

Washing Babies

OBJECTIVES

Emotional | Children will learn how to show affection.

Social | Children will take on adult roles, demonstrating a desire to grow up.

Diversity | Children will be exposed to different skin colors.

MATERIALS

Baby changing materials, such as empty powder and lotion bottles,
balance scales, towels, and diapers

Baby clothes

Soapy water (about 3 or 4 squirts of Joy or Dawn dishwashing soap works the best)

Bathing materials, such as washcloths, sponges, small bars of soap,
and empty trial-sized shampoo bottles

Multicultural baby dolls

Rocking chair, lullaby music, and baby board books, optional

SETTING UP THE ACTIVITY

1. Make a changing table out of blocks or dramatic play equipment. Put changing materials and baby clothes on the changing table.
2. Put the sand and water table near the changing table and fill it with soapy water.
3. Add a few of the bathing materials.
4. Give the children multicultural baby dolls and encourage them to give the dolls a bath. When finished bathing his baby, each child can change his doll and dress it.
5. If desired, put a rocking chair, lullaby music, and baby board books nearby for the children to use to put their dolls to sleep.

MULTICULTURAL DOLLS

EMPTY TRIAL-SIZE SHAMPOO BOTTLE

WASHCLOTH

LITTLE BAR OF SOAP

SPONGE

Tips

Ask the parents (send a note home, post a notice outside the classroom door, or put a note in a newsletter) to bring in empty containers of baby products. It is important to be resourceful when acquiring materials.

Open-Ended Questions

What makes babies happy?

When you are a parent, how will you take care of your baby?

How does it make you feel when you are taking care of your baby?

Spotlight Words
Caring
Comfort
Compassion
Empathy
Loving
Soft
Tender

Plant Nursery

OBJECTIVES

Intellectual | Children will write numbers as they price the plants.

Literacy | Children will pretend to read the plant names.

Social | Children will divide their attention between playmates. (For example, playing alone, playing with one or two children, or playing with the majority of the group.)

MATERIALS

Silk or plastic plants and flowers

Clay or plastic pots

Plant flats

Potting soil

Small garden shovels

Popsicle sticks labeled with a variety of plant names (for example, fern and ivy)

Sticker labels

Pen or marker

Small watering cans

Cash register and play money

SETTING UP THE ACTIVITY

1. Move the sand and water table to a different part of the room and set up a plant shop.
2. Add the plant materials to the sand and water table. Encourage the children to plant the flowers and plants in the pots and flats. They can label them with the Popsicle sticks, if desired.
3. After they have potted their plants, the children can price them. Help them write prices on sticker labels.
4. The children can use a cash register and play money to buy and sell plants.

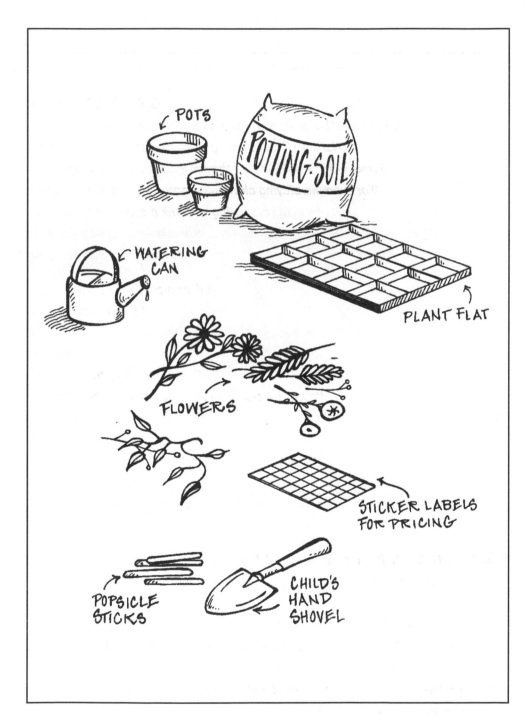

POTS

POTTING-SOIL

WATERING CAN

PLANT FLAT

FLOWERS

STICKER LABELS FOR PRICING

POPSICLE STICKS

CHILD'S HAND SHOVEL

Tips
Let the children decide the price of the plants.

Open-Ended Questions
How much would you sell this plant for?

Why does this plant cost more than that one?

Why do you water plants?

What happens when a plant isn't watered?

Spotlight Words
All
Less
More
Most
None
Same

Fossils

OBJECTIVES

Intellectual | Children will learn about paleontology and what a fossil is. Children will guess what is hidden in the plaster of Paris.
Literacy | Children will enhance their visual discrimination skills.
Emotional | Children will complete a project they start.
Physical | Children will develop their fine motor skills.
Diversity | Children will accept non-traditional roles by seeing that men and women can be paleontologists.

MATERIALS

Small figures, such as dinosaur figures, bones, shells, and so on
Plaster of Paris
Sand, rocks, or pebbles
Plastic knives or Popsicle sticks
Paper
Markers and crayons

SETTING UP THE ACTIVITY

1. Create homemade fossils by placing small figures in plaster of Paris. Allow the plaster to harden overnight.
2. Place these plaster of Paris-covered figures in the sand and water table and cover them with sand, rocks, or pebbles.
3. Give the children plastic knives or Popsicle sticks (or any safe tool in your environment). Review the rules about knives. Encourage them to chip away the plaster of Paris from the object.
4. When the children have chipped away enough plaster of Paris to partially expose the object, ask them to stop and draw what they have exposed. The children will then predict what is still hidden and complete their drawing using their imagination.

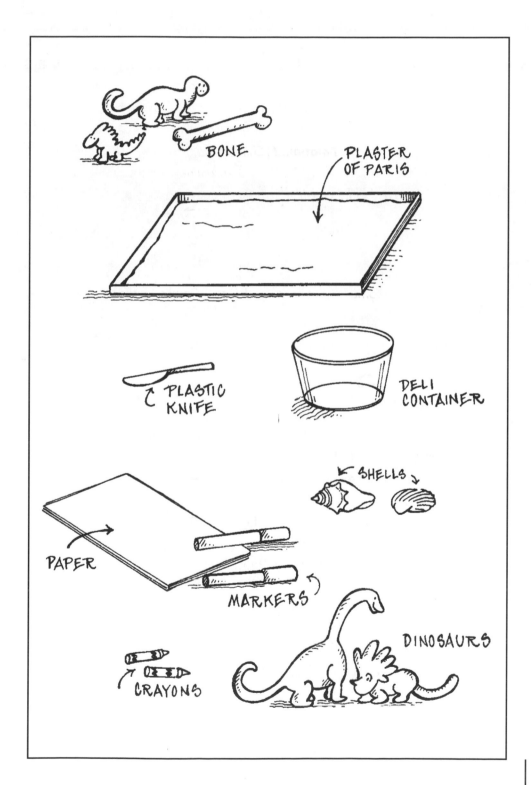

BONE

PLASTER OF PARIS

PLASTIC KNIFE

DELI CONTAINER

PAPER

MARKERS

SHELLS

CRAYONS

DINOSAURS

Open-Ended Questions

How are we going to find what is hidden?

What do you think we are going to do?

Spotlight Words

Discover
Examine
Fossil
Paleontologist
Predict

Environment Activities

Construction Workers 36

Astronauts 38

Marine Dock 40

Snow 42

Cars and Airplanes 44

Digging for Dinos 46

Homey Habitats 48

Construction Workers

OBJECTIVES

Literacy | Children will be exposed to environmental print and understand symbols in their world.

Social | Children will discuss different goals with their peers and coordinate to a common goal.

Diversity | Children will appreciate diversity in regards to gender roles.

MATERIALS

Poster board

Markers

Popsicle sticks

Glue

Small rocks

Sand

Hard hats

Small plastic trucks and bulldozers

SETTING UP THE ACTIVITY

1. With the children, make construction signs using markers and poster board, then glue the signs to Popsicle sticks. Examples of signs are: Construction Ahead, Detour, Slow, Stop, and so on. (See examples on pages 117-118.)

2. Put small rocks and sand in the sand and water table. Add small plastic trucks and bulldozers and encourage the children to pretend to be construction workers.

DETOUR

CONSTRUCTION AHEAD

SLOW

BULLDOZER

STOP

↑ HARD HAT

ROCK ↗

SAND ↑

Astronauts

OBJECTIVES

Intellectual | Children will understand the differences between reality and fantasy by talking about things that are real or not real in space.

Emotional | Children will gain an awareness of their own feelings and be able to verbalize them.

Social | Children will enter ongoing play.

MATERIALS

Rock salt

Small astronaut figures

Rocks about 5" – 7" (12 cm – 17 cm) in diameter

Space shuttles

Moon vehicles and toys

SETTING UP THE ACTIVITY

1. Pour rock salt in the sand and water table. Add the rest of the materials and encourage the children to pretend to be in space.

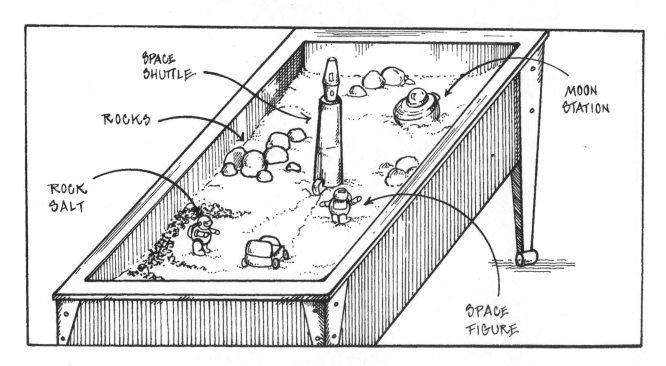

SPACE
SHUTTLE

ROCKS

ROCK
SALT

MOON
STATION

SPACE
FIGURE

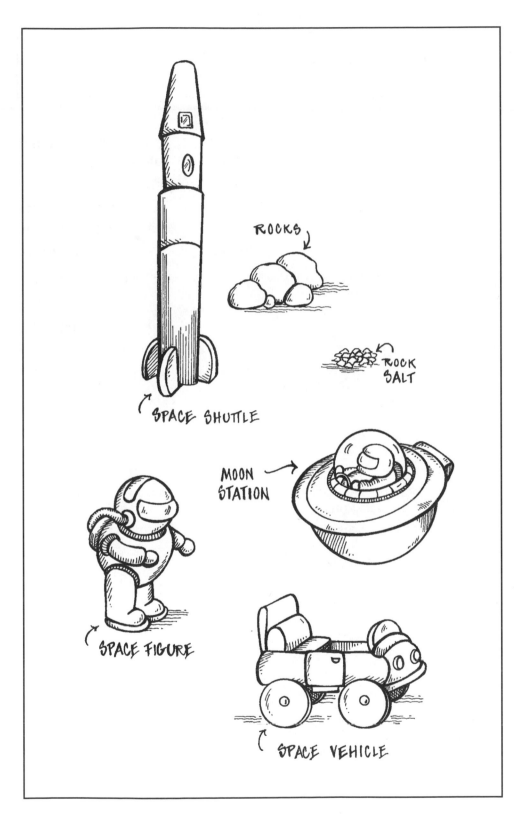

ROCKS

ROCK SALT

SPACE SHUTTLE

MOON STATION

SPACE FIGURE

SPACE VEHICLE

Open-Ended Questions

How do you feel about taking a trip to the moon?

What do you think it is like on the moon?

How long do you think it will take to get to the moon?

What does an astronaut do?

Spotlight Words
Astronaut
Cold
Craters
Earth
Far
Hot
Moon
Near
Stars
Sun

Marine Dock

OBJECTIVES

Literacy | Children will have the opportunity to play alone or in small groups.

Emotional | Children will have the chance to soothe away their frustrations and angry feelings.

Social | Children will verbalize their needs and ideas to adults and peers.

MATERIALS

Plastic boats

Multicultural people figures

Shells

Coral

Large piece of flat Styrofoam or cork (to make a dock)

Small plastic fish

Water

SETTING UP THE ACTIVITY

1. Put all the materials in the sand and water table.
2. Add water and encourage the children to interact with the materials and with each other.

BOATS

CORAL

SHELLS

FISH

Tips
When you add people figures to this activity, it becomes much more meaningful to the children. They start to take on roles and create play situations.

Open-Ended Questions
What things would a sea diver find under the ocean?

Who could you ask to play with you?

Spotlight Words
Above
Below
Diver
Dock
Float
In
Ocean
Out
Sink

Snow

OBJECTIVES

Emotional | *Children will be encouraged to put their own ideas into action.*

Social | *Children will consider the rights and feelings of others by respecting other people's ideas and possessions.*

Physical | *Children will increase their small motor skills.*

MATERIALS

Snow

Gloves

Ice cube trays

Food coloring

Freezer

Large buttons, Popsicle sticks, strips of fabric

Small containers

Eyedroppers

Sand molds

Small sand shovels

Multicultural people

Small plastic penguins, polar bears, seals, and walruses

SETTING UP THE ACTIVITY

1. Fill the sand and water table with clean snow. Make sure the children wear their gloves when playing with the snow, so their hands won't get cold.

   Snow Blocks—Fill ice cube trays with water and add food coloring to each cube. Place the trays in a freezer. (It takes about a week to prepare the ice cubes.) Add the colored snow blocks to the snow and encourage the children to build with them.

   Miniature Snow People—Encourage the children to make snow people by attaching large buttons, Popsicle sticks, and strips of fabric to snow balls.

   Colored Snow—Fill small containers with colored water (water and food coloring). Encourage the children to use eyedroppers to transfer the colored water to the snow to make colored snow.

Snow Castles—The children can make snow castles using snow, sand molds, and small sand shovels. Encourage them to add multicultural people figures to the castles.

Antarctic—Add small plastic penguins, polar bears, seals, walruses, and multicultural people figures. Encourage the children to pretend to be in Antarctica.

Cars and Airplanes

OBJECTIVES

Literacy | Children will expand their vocabulary and grammar by speaking in sentences, asking questions, and taking turns in conversations.

Social | Children will pay attention and listen to other children's ideas, make social initiations, and respect personal space.

MATERIALS

Sand or small rocks
Plastic cars and trucks
Airplanes
Multicultural people figures

SETTING UP THE ACTIVITY

1. Fill the sand and water table half full with sand or small rocks. Add cars, trucks, airplanes, and multicultural people figures to it and encourage the children to experiment.

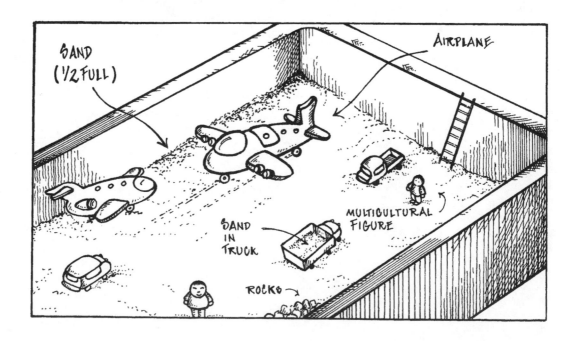

Tips

Allow the children to reject each other's ideas and the teacher's help with respect. Children will learn the skills to interact appropriately by using other children's names, making eye contact, and touching the person respectfully. Children will function at increasingly higher levels of play.
(The four levels of play are:
parallel play—plays beside but not with others;
interactive play—beginning social interaction;
associative play—play is loosely related with some interaction but not with shared goals; and
cooperative play—plays together with shared goals.)

Open-Ended Questions

Who could you ask to play with you?

Could you work together to solve this problem?

Spotlight Words

Airport
Down
Glider
Propeller
Runway
Up

Digging for Dinos

OBJECTIVES

Intellectual | Children will learn correct dinosaur names.
Children will classify dinosaur traits, such as meat eater vs. plant eater, with horns vs. without, two-legged vs. four-legged, large vs. small, and so on.

Literacy | Children will read books that provide factual information about dinosaurs.

Emotional | Children will channel their aggressive behavior from fighting to nurturing by having dinosaur families that care for each other.

Social | Children will take turns playing with different dinosaurs.
Children will role-play different family roles such as Mom, Dad, baby, Grandpa, aunt, and so on.

Diversity | Children will see that dinosaurs have some characteristics that are the same, but also have differences—just like people.
Children will identify different kinds of family units.

MATERIALS

Colored aquarium rocks
Plastic tablecloth, optional
Large and small plastic dinosaurs
Plastic eggs
Plastic plants
Cardboard packing corners (for dinosaur homes)
Containers of water, optional

SETTING UP THE ACTIVITY

1. Place colored aquarium rocks in the bottom of the sand and water table. If desired, line the sand and water table with a plastic tablecloth that has scenery on it before placing the aquarium rocks in it.

2. Put the other materials in the sand and water table and encourage the children to play.

3. Add containers of water to make lakes, rivers, and oceans, if desired.

Plastic Egg

Plastic Plant

Cardboard Packing Corner

Dinosaurs

Colored Aquarium Rocks

Tips

By adding smaller dinosaurs and plastic eggs with larger dinosaurs, the children will be motivated to create families, friends, and so on.

Remember how important it is to let children play with equipment as long as their interest in playing continues. Often teachers force children to give up equipment before they are ready. Children are creatively stifled, unable to work through situations, or complete their play when this occurs. Also, provide enough equipment so there will be fewer conflicts.

Open-Ended Questions

What can you find that is the same with all dinosaurs?

Is there another way that dinosaurs can behave?

Who is in your dinosaur family?
Is that the same as _____ family?

When you are finished playing with that dinosaur, do you think (another child's name) can play with it?

Spotlight Words

Angry
Classify
Cooperation
Different
Fairness
Function
Happy
Sad
Same
Shape
Size
Sort
Teamwork

Homey Habitats

FIGURE

ELEPHANT

FROG

STRAW

SNAKE

PLASTIC
CACTUS

LION

OBJECTIVES

Intellectual | Children will learn information about different habitats and the animals that live there.

Literacy | The children will verbally communicate with peers.

Emotional | Children will become involved in an activity where they can function apart from their parents.

Social | Children will pay attention and accept others' ideas, social initiations, and personal space.

Diversity | Children will be exposed to different cultures and skin colors by playing with multicultural people figures.

MATERIALS

A home and animals that relate to the habitat

Zoo

Plastic zoo animals • Toy trucks • Multicultural people figures • Legos or Lincoln logs (to make fences) • Colored rocks

Ocean

Plastic sea animals • Seashells • Colored water • Large broken up pieces of Styrofoam (to make icebergs)

Desert

Plastic lizards and snakes • Rocks • Plastic cacti • Sand

Farm

Plastic farm animals • Straw • Legos or Lincoln logs (to make fences) • Small barn • Small cups (to make feeding troughs)

Jungle

Plastic jungle animals • Plastic plants • Shredded green paper

Savannah

Small plastic animals, such as giraffes, lions, elephants, and zebras • Straw or dried grass clippings • Bowl with water (to make a water hole)

Ranch

Plastic horses • Sawdust • Legos or Lincoln logs (to make fences) • Multicultural people figures

Pond

Plastic frogs • Circles cut from flat cork (to make lily pads) • Plastic plants • Colored water • Aquarium rocks (optional)

SETTING UP THE ACTIVITY

1. Put the materials from one type of habitat in the sand and water table. (Add multicultural people with any habitat.)
2. Add sand, water, or another medium to the sand and water table.
3. Encourage the children to play.
4. Put out materials, people, and animals from another habitat on another day.

FARM ANIMAL

SEA ANIMAL

Tips

Place a tape recorder near the sand and water table as the children play. Later, play the tape and encourage the children to listen to help develop their listening skills and to generate ideas to create a story.

Adding people figures to the activity increases social interaction.

Open-Ended Questions

Do you have any other ideas?

How can we let _____ join into our play?

What would you do if you lived in this habitat?

If you were an a_____ what would you do a_____ day?

Spotlig

MULTICULTURAL FIGURES

Outdoors Activities

Backyard Beach Party 52

Sand Castles, Canals, and Tunnels 54

Sand Stew 56

Garden 58

Car Wash 60

Biggie Bubbles 62

Rainbow Maker 64

Backyard Beach Party

OBJECTIVES

Emotional | Children will act on their own ideas and build self-esteem.

Social | Children will cooperate with each other as they follow through with their plans.

MATERIALS

Two sand and water tables

Sand

Seashells

Plastic sea animals

Water

Toy boats

Multicultural people figures

Beach umbrella

Beach towels

Sunglasses and hats

Beach balls

SETTING UP THE ACTIVITY

1. Set up two sand and water tables outside. In one of the sand and water tables, add sand and seashells. In the other, add water, sea animals, and boats.
2. Set up a beach umbrella and beach towels nearby.
3. Give the children beach balls and encourage them to have a beach party.

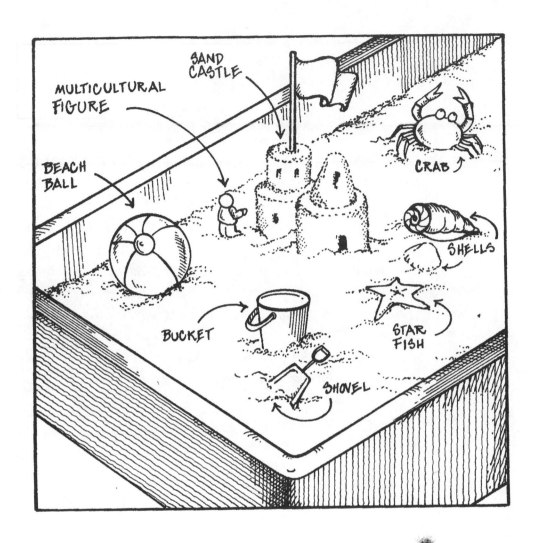

MULTICULTURAL FIGURE

SAND CASTLE

BEACH BALL

CRAB

SHELLS

BUCKET

STAR FISH

SHOVEL

Open-Ended Questions

Do you have any ideas?

Spotlight Words

Beach

Ocean

Sand

Shade

Shore

Tide

Waves

Sand Castles, Canals, and Tunnels

OBJECTIVES

Intellectual | Children will develop problem-solving skills as they create tunnels and canals for their sand castles.

Emotional | Children will build confidence and feel proud of their work as they create a sand castle.

Social | Children will show respect for their peers' work.

Physical | Children will develop eye-hand coordination.

MATERIALS

Sand

Water

Sand molds

Small shovels

Buckets

SETTING UP THE ACTIVITY

1. Bring the sand and water table outside.
2. Fill it with sand, water, and the other materials and encourage the children to create sand castles.

SHOVEL

BUCKET

MOLDS

Tips

Help the children make "Please Do Not Touch" signs and allow the castles to set for a few days. Younger children love to save their projects and return later to share it with their friends or family members. Teachers can also take snapshots to preserve their work. Put the photos in the classroom scrapbook and display it in the reading area.

Open-Ended Questions

Can you make a plan for a sand castle?

Do you feel good about your work?

Where does sand come from?

Where do you usually find sand?

Does sand hold its shape better when it's wet or dry?

Spotlight Words

Castle

Empty

Full

In

Out

Short

Tall

Sand Stew

OBJECTIVES

Intellectual | Children will identify objects in nature and respect the environment.

Literacy | Children will write creatively with the teacher's help.

Emotional | Children will have a tactile experience as they create their sand stew.

Social | Children will share their ideas as they work together.

MATERIALS

Objects from nature, such as rocks, sticks, leaf bits, dandelions, grass, and so on

Sand

Paint smocks

Water cans

Sticks

Paper and pens

SETTING UP THE ACTIVITY

1. Go outside with the children and help them gather the "ingredients" (objects from nature) to make sand stew.

2. Bring the sand and water table outside and pour sand into it.

3. Make sure the children wear their paint smocks for this activity. Encourage the children to add water and other ingredients to the sand. They can mix everything together using sticks.

4. Ask the children to create a recipe for their concoction. Write it down for them and create a class recipe book.

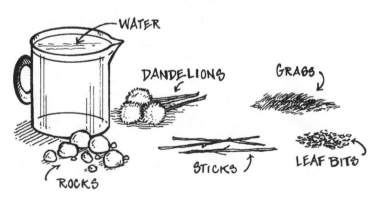

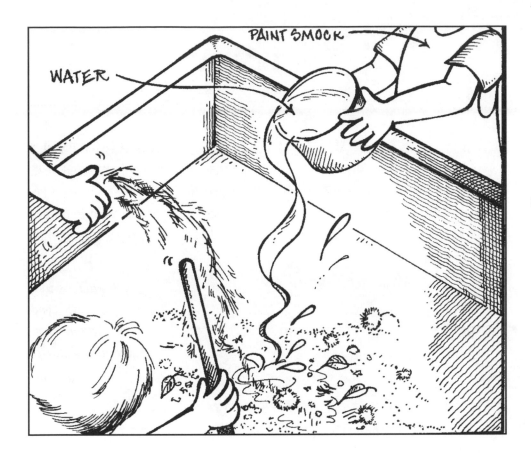

WATER

PAINT SMOCK

Tips

The children can learn to respect the environment at a very young age. Encourage the children to collect only the things they find on the ground that are not growing.

Open-Ended Questions

What do you think will happen when you mix water with the sand?

Will the sand melt?

How can you respect the world around you? Is wet sand heavier then dry sand?

How does wet sand look different then dry sand?

Spotlight Words
Life
Mix
Nature
Respect

Garden

OBJECTIVES

Intellectual | Children will learn facts about gardening and how things grow.

Social | Children will work together to create a garden.

MATERIALS

Dirt or sand

Gardening tools

Seeds

Watering cans

Plastic plants and flowers

SETTING UP THE ACTIVITY

1. Bring the sand and water table outside and place dirt or sand in the bottom of it.
2. Supply the children with gardening tools, seeds, watering cans, and plastic plants and flowers. Encourage the children to create and care for a garden in the sand and water table.

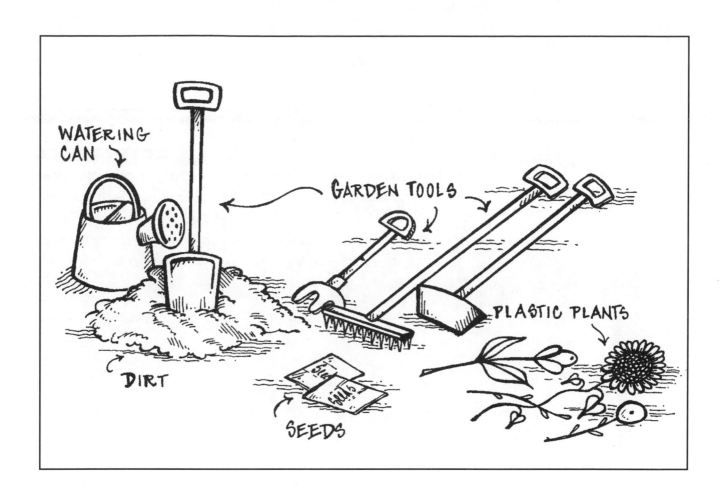

WATERING CAN

GARDEN TOOLS

PLASTIC PLANTS

DIRT

SEEDS

Open-Ended Questions	Spotlight Words
What happens to seeds when they are planted?	Grow
	Roots
	Seeds
	Sprout
What makes the seed grow?	Strong
	Weak
	Weeds
How can you take care of a garden?	

Car Wash

OBJECTIVES

Intellectual | Children will understand how to exchange money for services.

Literacy | Children will attempt to write using letter-like forms as they create "Open" and "Closed" signs for the car wash.

Physical | Children will enhance large motor skills as they ride trikes to the carwash.

Social | Children will show courtesy and respect towards others.

MATERIALS

Water

Buckets

Soap

Scrubbers

Rags and towels

Spray bottles

Trikes

Poster board

Markers

Play money

SETTING UP THE ACTIVITY

1. Bring the sand and water table outside and fill it with water.
2. Place the cleaning equipment in the bottom of it.
3. Help the children make signs and set up the car wash.
4. Encourage the children to ride their trikes to the car wash and wash them. The children can use play money to pay for a car wash.

SIGN

CAR WASH

TRIKE

BUCKET

SPRAY BOTTLE

TOWEL

SCRUBBER

PLAY MONEY

RAG

Open-Ended Questions

How can you get some friends to come to your car wash?

How much should a car wash cost?

Spotlight Words

Clean

Come again

Dirty

Money

Scrub

Service

Thank you

Biggie Bubbles

OBJECTIVES

Intellectual | Children will discover the science in bubbles by discovering how to make bubbles, watching the surface tension, and observing the bubbles float.

Emotional | Children will have the opportunity to soothe away their frustrations and angry feelings by being involved in a sensorimotor activity.

Physical | Children will increase their large motor skills and coordination as they chase the bubbles.

MATERIALS

Hardy Bubbles recipe (page 121)

Large bubble wands

Hula hoops

Soothing, calming music

Videotape recorder and blank tape

SETTING UP THE ACTIVITY

1. Use the Hardy Bubbles recipe on page 121 to make bubbles.
2. Put the bubbles into the sand and water table and bring it outside.
3. Place large bubble wands in the sand and water table and play music to encourage the children to blow and chase the bubbles. Use hula hoops to make really big bubbles!
4. If desired, videotape the children playing and then play it back for them the next day.

HARDY BUBBLE RECIPE

BIGGIE BUBBLE

BUBBLE WANDS

Tips

Sometimes the simplest activities are the ones the children enjoy the most.

Open-Ended Questions

Why do you think bubbles float?

How many colors can you find in a bubble?

Are bubbles science?

Spotlight Words

Colors
Down
Float
In
Out
Pop
Rise
Sink
Transparent
Up

Rainbow Maker

OBJECTIVES

Intellectual | Children learn that a rainbow is science.
(What conditions have to happen for a rainbow to form?)
Literacy | Children will have an opportunity to be read to.
Social | Children will work together and discuss their conclusions with each other.

MATERIALS

A Rainbow of My Own by Don Freeman
Hose with a sprinkler
Multicultural people figures
Small containers
Mirrors (to reflect light)

SETTING UP THE ACTIVITY

1. Read *A Rainbow of My Own* by Don Freeman. This book will help stimulate discussions about rainbows. Rainbows are one of the children's favorite things to paint, draw, talk about, and search for.

2. Bring the sand and water table outside. Turn a sprinkler on low and place it in the table.

3. Put the multicultural people figures, small containers, and mirrors in the sand and water table.

4. If necessary, help the children create a rainbow.

5. Name the colors of the rainbow. Show the children that there is an order in the colors of a rainbow (red, orange, yellow, green, blue, and violet). Explain that sunlight is made up of all colors.

6. Talk about the conditions that are necessary to make a rainbow.

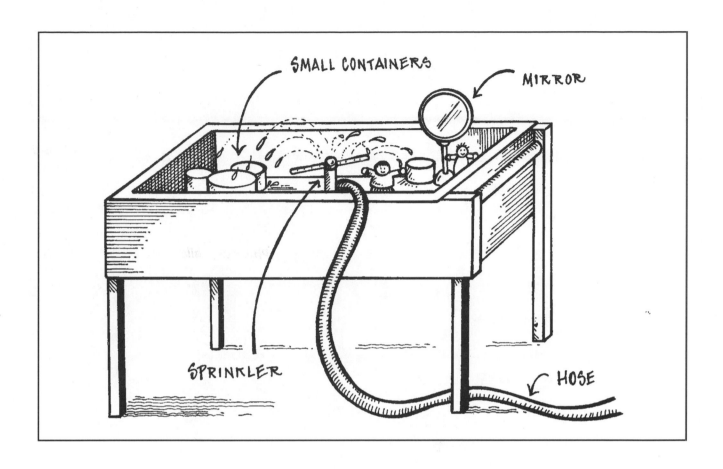

SMALL CONTAINERS

MIRROR

SPRINKLER

HOSE

Tips

Children at a young age are not likely to come to correct conclusions about how rainbows are made, or even to recall the color order. But doing science activities arouses children's curiosity and gives them a sense of the world around them. It is not important that they understand the scientific concepts; it is the process of discovery that is important.

Open-Ended Questions

What happens when it rains?

What happens when the sun is shining and it rains?

Where do rainbows come from?

What colors do you see?

Spotlight Words

Color prisms
Light
Order
Over
Rain
Reflect
Shine
Under

Science Activities

Air Moves Things 68

Magnets 70

See and Feel 72

Float and Sink 74

Melting Pot 76

Oobleck 78

Vinegar and Baking Soda 80

Ice Cubes 82

Air and Water Wonders 84

Test Tubes 86

Air Moves Things

OBJECTIVES

Intellectual | Children will learn that air is real and can move things.
Children will learn about cause and effect.
Emotional | Children will try a new and different activity.

MATERIALS

Light objects such as Ping-Pong balls, feathers, pieces of tissue paper, leaves,
Styrofoam packing, rocks, and cotton balls
Straws
Masking tape
Marker

SETTING UP THE ACTIVITY

1. Place the objects in the sand and water table.
2. Give each child her own straw. Use masking tape and a marker to label each child's straw. Make sure the children do not share straws. This will keep the activity sanitary and prevent the spread of germs from one child to another.
3. Encourage the children to experiment blowing the different objects using their straws.

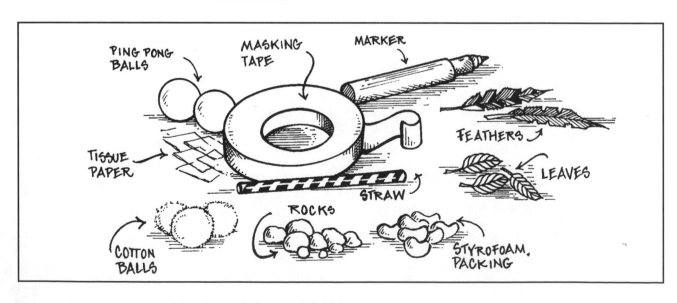

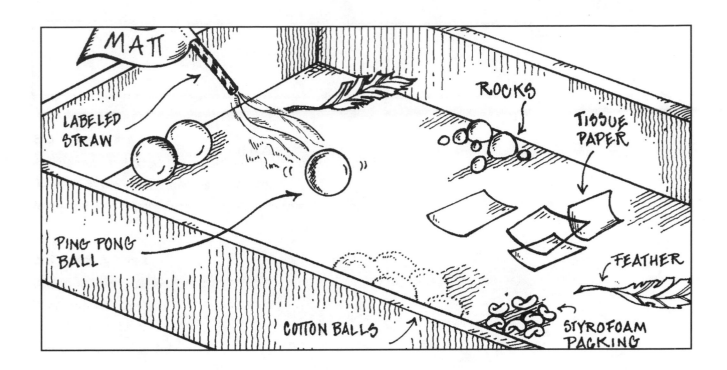

MATT

LABELED STRAW

PING PONG BALL

ROCKS

TISSUE PAPER

FEATHER

COTTON BALLS

STYROFOAM PACKING

Open-Ended Questions

If air is invisible, how do we know that it is all around us?

What happens to the objects when you blow on them?

How can you tell which direction the wind blows?

Spotlight Words

Air

Heavy

Light

Move

Wind

Magnets

OBJECTIVES

Intellectual | *Children will generate options and solutions, discuss them, and try out their ideas.*

Social | *Children will work together towards a common goal.*

MATERIALS

Magnets, in a variety of sizes

Small metal objects

Small plastic objects

Small wooden objects

Sand or another medium (see list on page 11)

SETTING UP THE ACTIVITY

1. Place metal, plastic, and wooden objects in the sand and water table.
2. Give the children magnets and encourage them to experiment to see which items the magnets will attract.
3. Cover the objects with sand or another medium.
4. Encourage the children to have a magnetic treasure hunt.

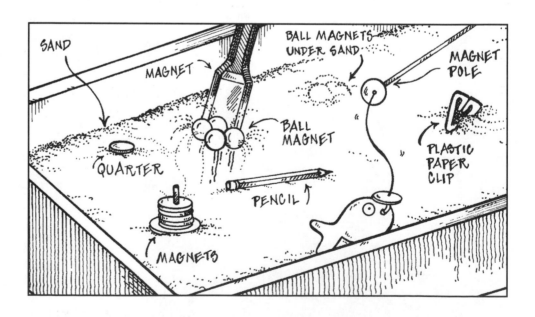

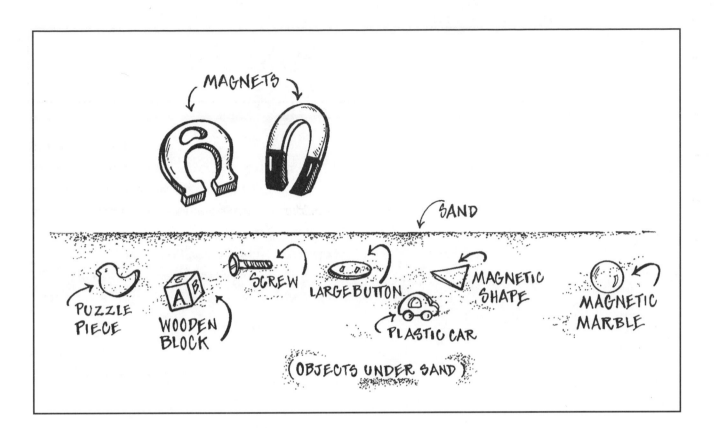

Open-Ended Questions

What else would you do with these magnets?

Would you show me what you have done here?

Tips

When you join the children who have been experimenting in the sand and water table, ask open-ended questions. Do not assume certain results or conclusions. Ask, "Would you show me what you have done?"

Spotlight Words

Attract
Close
Far
Large
Magnetize
Repel
Small

See and Feel

OBJECTIVES

Intellectual | Children will distinguish between different textures through sight and touch.
Children will expand their vocabulary by learning new words to describe textures.
Literacy | Children will create books using their texture rubbings.
Emotional | Children will use their creativity by putting their own ideas into action.
Children will try a new and different activity.
Social | Children will be encouraged to verbalize with teachers and peers.

MATERIALS

Objects with defined textures, such as Legos, leaves, shells, coins,
smooth plates, corrugated cardboard, or plastic trays
Construction paper
Fat, peeled crayons
Cardboard
Glue or paste
Hole punch
String
Markers

SETTING UP THE ACTIVITY

1. Place the various objects in the sand and water table. Encourage the children to look at, feel, and describe the objects.
2. Put construction paper over the objects. Show the children how to make rubbings by rubbing crayons over the paper-covered objects. Encourage the children to talk about the different textures.
3. Help each child make a texture book. Ask the children to paste lightweight samples of various textured materials, such as cotton balls, sandpaper, feathers, or pieces of fabric, onto cardboard. Ask the children to choose rubbings to add to their books. Put all of the pages together and punch three holes along the right side of the book (teacher only). Attach the book

together using string. Encourage the children to describe the characteristics of their rubbings. Write down their descriptions on each page (or encourage the children to do it if they are able).

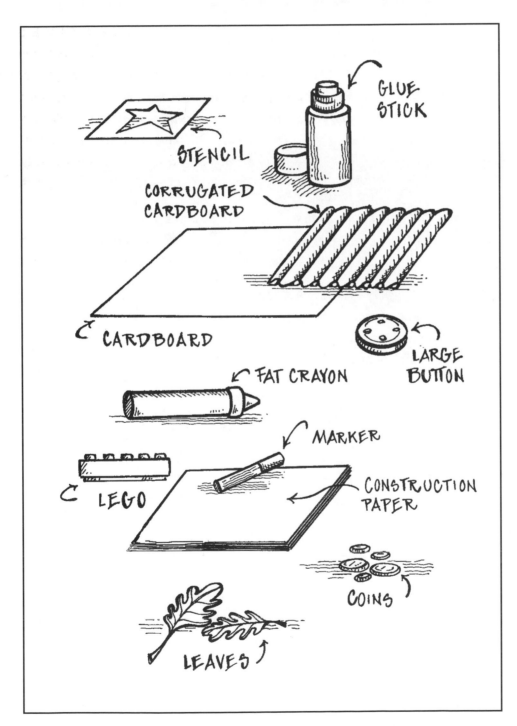

GLUE STICK

STENCIL

CORRUGATED CARDBOARD

CARDBOARD

LARGE BUTTON

FAT CRAYON

MARKER

LEGO

CONSTRUCTION PAPER

COINS

LEAVES

Open-Ended Questions

What does it feel like?

What does your rubbing remind you of?

What can you tell me about your book?

Spotlight Words
Bumpy
Hard
Line
Rough
Round
Shape
Smooth
Soft
Texture

Float and Sink

OBJECTIVES

Intellectual | *Children will make guesses about possible outcomes, try out different solutions, and observe results.*
Literacy | *Children will verbalize their thoughts as the teacher records them.*
Social | *Children will work together towards a common goal.*

MATERIALS

Water
Objects that will sink and float, such as paper clips, little pieces of wood, nuts and bolts, Styrofoam, and so on

SETTING UP THE ACTIVITY

1. Fill the sand and water table about ¾ full of water.
2. Encourage the children to experiment with the different objects to see if they will sink or float.

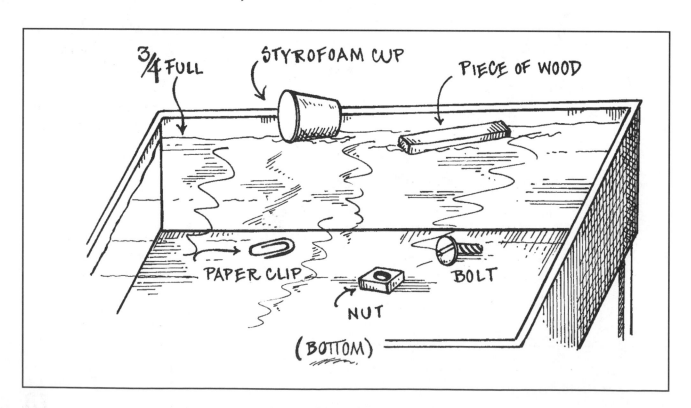

Open-Ended Questions

What can you do with these objects?

What can you do now?

Tips

A teacher must use good judgment when answering questions. Avoid the temptation to tell children the answer. Giving children quick answers may cause them to lose confidence because they are afraid to be wrong. More important, though, is that quick answers cheat children out of discovering for themselves. Answer questions directly only if a child cannot get the answer for herself.

Spotlight Words
Drop
Float
On top of
Sink
Under

Melting Pot

OBJECTIVES

Intellectual | Children will identify and examine the items they use.
Literacy | Children will describe and verbalize what is happening.
Social | Children will verbalize and have a conversation with their peers.

MATERIALS

Objects to melt, such as crayons, birthday candles,
large candles, ice cubes, chocolate bars, or snow
Foil
Warming trays

SETTING UP THE ACTIVITY

Note: Supervise this activity at all times.

1. Ask the children to identify and examine the objects before placing them in the sand and water table.

2. Line the sand and water table with foil for easy cleanup. Place warming trays in the sand and water table.
   Note: Use warming trays because they do not get too hot. Burners, however, are not safe to use in this activity!

3. Place foil on top of the warming trays. Then, place the objects to melt on top of the foil.

4. Encourage the children to observe the objects change and describe what happens. Record their thoughts and observations.

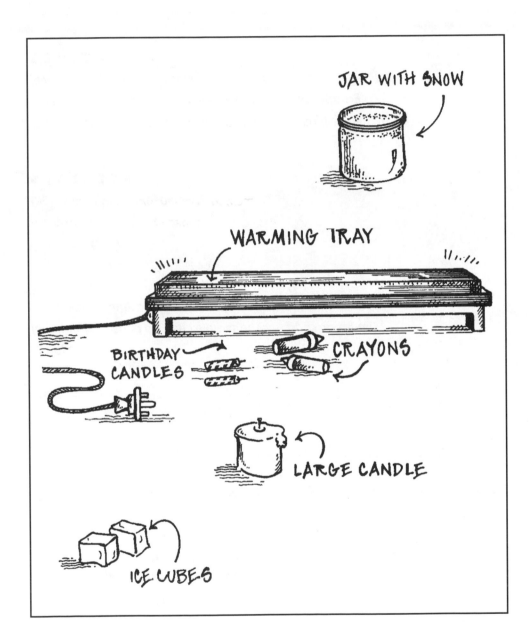

JAR WITH SNOW

WARMING TRAY

BIRTHDAY CANDLES

CRAYONS

LARGE CANDLE

ICE CUBES

Open-Ended Questions

What happens?

Why do you think the change occurred?

Spotlight Words

Change
Color
Fast
Melt
Shape
Size
Slow

Oobleck

OBJECTIVES

Intellectual | Children will observe a substance change from a solid to a liquid.

Emotional | Children will release tension in a positive way.

Social | Children will be accepted by other children in the group.

MATERIALS

Recipe for oobleck (page 122)

Cornstarch

Measuring cups

Water

Containers

Washable liquid paint

Prediction chart (see the sample chart on page 114), optional

Food coloring

Gelatin

Bowl and spoon

Clean, empty margarine containers

Ice cubes

SETTING UP THE ACTIVITY

1. Look at the recipe for oobleck on page 122. Measure the cornstarch (according to the recipe) and place it in the bottom of the sand and water table. Pour the correct amount of water into a container and put it to the side. Then, ask the children to mix the water with the cornstarch. Add washable liquid paint. If desired, use a prediction chart to record the children's predictions and discoveries.

2. Try one of the following ideas:

   Food Coloring—Instead of using washable liquid paint, add food coloring to the oobleck. Encourage the children to make different colors and designs.

Individual Portions—After the children have experienced playing with oobleck, ask them to mix their own individual portions of oobleck. In separate containers, encourage the children to experiment with the amount of cornstarch and water and observe the results.

Solid or Liquid?—Oobleck can also be a good catalyst to begin talking about different things that are a solid or a liquid. One activity that helps children understand the concept of changing from a liquid to a solid is to make Jell-O. Empty a packet of gelatin into a bowl and stir in boiling water. Pour a small amount into individual margarine containers for each child. Add ice cubes to the liquid gelatin. Encourage the children to observe long enough to watch the Jell-O dissolve in the hot water and set.

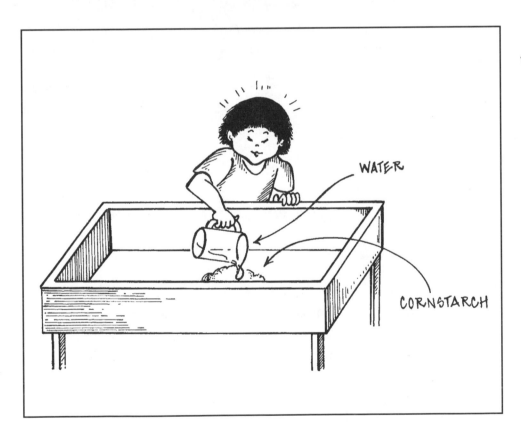

WATER

CORNSTARCH

Tips
Books and group time make great springboard activities for sand and water table activities. For example, read *Bartholomew and the Oobleck* by Dr. Seuss before experimenting with oobleck in the sand and water table.

Open-Ended Questions
What changes do you see in the cornstarch after adding the water?

What happened?

What did we observe?

Spotlight Words
Angry
Happy
Liquid
Melt
Smooth
Soft
Solid

Vinegar and Baking Soda

OBJECTIVES

Intellectual | Children will understand cause and effect. Children will make a guess about and try out possible outcomes, observe results, and draw conclusions.

Literacy | Children will understand the relationship between thoughts, spoken words, writing, and reading.

Social | Children will consider the rights of others by respecting their ideas.

MATERIALS

Two large containers

Vinegar

Baking soda

Clear plastic cups and containers

Prediction chart (see the sample chart on page 114)

Measuring cups

SETTING UP THE ACTIVITY

1. Pour vinegar into one large container and baking soda into the other large container. Place both containers in the sand and water table.

2. Place clear plastic cups and containers in the sand and water table and encourage the children to experiment mixing the two materials. Use a prediction chart (see page 114), if desired.

3. Encourage the children to use measuring cups to measure the amount they need.

LARGE CONTAINERS

Vinegar

MEASURING CUPS

Baking Soda

FOOD COLORING

CLEAR PLASTIC CUPS

Open-Ended Questions

Tell me what you think might happen?

What have we done so far?

How does it work?

Tips

When teaching science, it is very important to remember to validate any conclusion a child comes up with, whether it is "right" or not. Science is a process of discovery, and the teacher's role is to question and guide the children through the process. At the end of the activity, if the teacher can say the child has learned something, then it has been successful.

Spotlight Words
Change
Measure
Mix
Reaction

Ice Cubes

OBJECTIVES

Intellectual | Children will use the scientific method (observing, predicting, experimenting, and so on).

Children will discover cause and effect.

Children will learn how different things melt.

Literacy | Children will have the opportunity to verbalize and write as they predict outcomes.

Emotional | Children will try new and different activities.

Social | Children will work together towards a common goal.

Tips

Encourage the children to make the decisions about the experiment. For example, ask them, "What are we going to freeze the water in? What should we add to the water?" Also, help the children record their own findings.

MATERIALS

Variety of molds, such as Jell-O molds, ice cream buckets, letter molds, candy and popcorn molds, and ice cube trays

Water

Food coloring

Various materials chosen by children, such as flowers, plants, and rocks

Prediction chart (see the sample chart on page 114)

Squirt bottles with warm water

Popsicle sticks or plastic knives

Rock salt

SETTING UP THE ACTIVITY

1. This activity is a two-day process. The first day, the children will prepare the water to freeze. The second day, the children will observe and experiment with the melting ice.

2. Encourage the children to add water to various molds.

3. To modify the activity, add food coloring and/or add objects, such as flowers, plants, or rocks, before freezing the water.

4. Place the molds in the freezer overnight to allow the water to freeze.

5. The next day, remove the molds from the freezer and place them in the sand and water table.

6. There are several different ways to melt the ice:

- Fill squirt bottles with warm water and squirt the ice.
- Use Popsicle sticks or plastic knives to chip away the ice. (Remember to review the rules about how to use the knives safely.)
- Put 1" to 2" (2 to 5 cm) of water in the bottom of the sand and water table.
- Put rock salt in the bottom of the sand and water table.

5. Use a prediction chart with the class. (See the sample chart on page 114.)

FOOD COLORING

JELLO MOLD

MARBLES

CANDY MOLD

PARSLEY

ICE CREAM BUCKET

FLOWERS

LETTER MOLDS

Open-Ended Questions

What happens when we put the water in the freezer?

What happens when we add salt to the water?

How many ways can you mix _____ with _____?

How many things can you add to this water that will make it change?

Spotlight Words

Blend
Cold
Dissolve
Fast
Freeze
Hot
Liquid
Melt
Mix
Slow
Solid
Thaw

Air and Water Wonders

OBJECTIVES

Intellectual | Children will discover that air is all around them and it pushes on things.

Social | Children will have the opportunity to work alone or in a group.

MATERIALS

Water

Paper towels

Clear plastic glasses with straight sides

Index cards

Food coloring

Plastic tubing

2 plastic syringes

SETTING UP THE ACTIVITY

1. Demonstrate each of the following science experiments for the children before asking them to experiment for themselves at the sand and water table.

   Paper Towel Experiment—Fill the sand and water table ¾ full with water. Place a paper towel into a clear plastic glass so that it is completely inside the cup. Place the glass upside down in the sand and water table and hold it under the water for a minute. Ask the children if they think the paper is completely soaked. Then, remove the glass and ask the children to touch the paper. Ask them, "Is it dry?"

   Note: Make sure the glass isn't tilted when you plunge it into the water. The air pressure inside the cup should keep the paper dry while it is in the water.

   Index Card Experiment—Fill a plastic glass with water. Place an index card over the top of the glass and hold it tightly over the lip of the cup. Invert the entire glass. Carefully remove the hand that was holding the card. The card should stay on the glass and no water should spill out.

   Note: Be sure to do this experiment over the sand and water table. Sometimes the card falls out too soon.

Plastic Tubing Experiment—Add food coloring to water to make colored water. Pour the colored water into a piece of plastic tubing. Connect two plastic syringes on either end of the piece of plastic tubing. Push in on the plunger of one syringe. What happens to the plunger of the other? Encourage the children to investigate this syringe system. (The air pressure inside the tubing should force the plungers to move.)

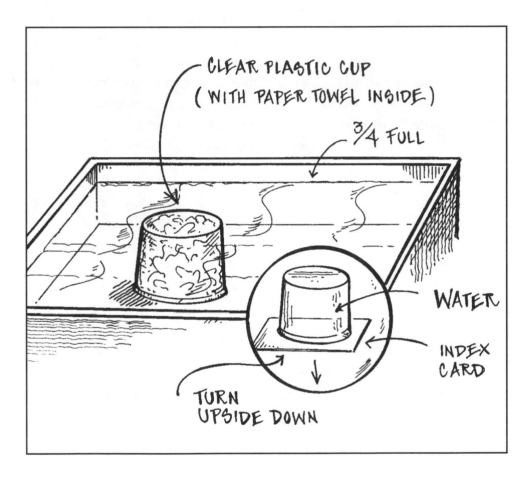

CLEAR PLASTIC CUP
(WITH PAPER TOWEL INSIDE)

¾ FULL

WATER

INDEX CARD

TURN UPSIDE DOWN

Test Tubes

OBJECTIVES

Intellectual | *Children will learn how to mix together different solutions and will learn the vocabulary of a chemist. Children will explore how to create colors by mixing them together. Children will predict, test, and observe possible outcomes.*

Literacy | *Children will have opportunities to use written symbols.*

Social | *Children will verbalize information to peers and adults.*

Physical | *Children will develop fine motor skills and eye-hand coordination.*

Diversity | *Children will see that boys and girls have non-traditional jobs and responsibilities. (For example, girls can be scientists.)*

MATERIALS

Lab coats (or adult-size short sleeve shirts)

Washable liquid paint

Water

Plastic bowls

Plastic test tubes

Eyedroppers

Coffee filters

Clipboards and pencils (For recording information on the clipboards, see an example of a prediction chart on page 114.)

SETTING UP THE ACTIVITY

1. Make sure the children wear lab coats for this activity.
2. Make colored water by adding washable liquid paint to water. Make the primary colors (red, yellow, and blue) and make sure the colors are dark enough to mix well. Pour each color into separate plastic bowls.
3. Pour white and black paint into separate bowls for the children to use to create different shades of color.
4. Place the bowls of colored water and paint, test tubes, and eyedroppers into the sand and water table. Encourage the children to use eyedroppers to mix the colors in the test tubes.

5. Another idea to try is:

   Coffee Filters—Place coffee filters in the bottom of the sand and water table. Ask the children to use the eyedroppers to drop the colored water onto the filters and observe the absorbency. They will also enjoy watching the colors move and mix.

6. If recording results, reproduce one prediction chart for each child (see page 114). Chart all the children's predictions on a separate graph.

(see page 114)

Open-Ended Questions

What will happen when we put two different colors together?

How many ways can you mix this color?

Spotlight Words

Chemicals
Color
Conclusions
Dark
Hue
Light
Mixing
Pale
Results
Shades
Solutions
Tint
Vibrant

Water Activities

Dump and Fill 90

Waterwheels 92

Legos and Water 94

Tongs and Balls 96

Boats 98

Pipes and Accordian Tubing 100

Dump and Fill

OBJECTIVES

Intellectual | Children will predict the amount of cups or spoons of water that it will take to fill the containers. Children will count the cupfuls or spoonfuls of water needed to fill the containers using tally sheets, counting, or another method. Children will understand the representation of number symbols.

Emotional | Children will release tension and become absorbed in an activity.

Social | Children will work together to predict outcomes and tally information by having one child tallying and another child counting full water cups. Children will work together to fill the containers.

Physical | Children will develop eye-hand coordination by pouring water into the containers.

MATERIALS

Dishwashing soap (Joy or Dawn works the best)
Water
Washable liquid paint
Tall, clear plastic containers in a variety of sizes
Measuring cups and spoons
Funnels
Tally cards
Syringes, tubing, eyedroppers, and other materials

SETTING UP THE ACTIVITY

1. Fill the sand and water table with 2"- 5" (5 cm -12 cm) of water. Squeeze three squirts of liquid dishwashing soap into water.
2. Color the water with liquid washable paint, such as Liquid Watercolors. Avoid using food coloring because it will stain the children's clothes and hands.
3. Encourage the children to dump and fill the various containers with water.
4. Ask the children to count how many cups or spoons it takes to fill a container using measuring cups and spoons and funnels. Help them keep

track of their counting by using tally cards. (See the example on page 115.)

5. Add syringes, tubing, eyedroppers, and other materials so the children can experiment with suction.

6. Try this activity using another medium, such as sand, acorns, or large buttons.

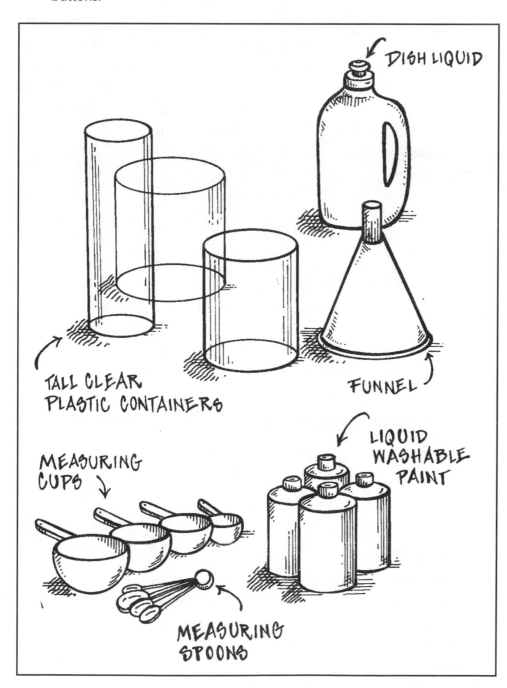

DISH LIQUID

TALL CLEAR
PLASTIC CONTAINERS

FUNNEL

MEASURING
CUPS

LIQUID
WASHABLE
PAINT

MEASURING
SPOONS

Tips
If you write every child's name on the class tally chart, each child will want to be a part of the activity.

Open-Ended Questions
How many cups do you think it will take to fill this container?

Who can you find to help you fill your container or tally your card?

Whose container has the most/least amount of water?

Spotlight Words
Cooperate
Empty
Full
Help
Less
More

Waterwheels

OBJECTIVES

Intellectual | Children will discover cause and effect
relationships as they use waterwheels.
Social | Children will be encouraged to work together.

MATERIALS

Sand, water, or another medium
Waterwheels
Scoops
Other supplies (see list of supply suggestions on page 11)

SETTING UP THE ACTIVITY

1. Pour your choice of a medium into the sand and water table to a depth of about 4" (10 cm) deep.
2. Place waterwheels, scoops, and any other supplies in the sand and water table and encourage the children to explore.

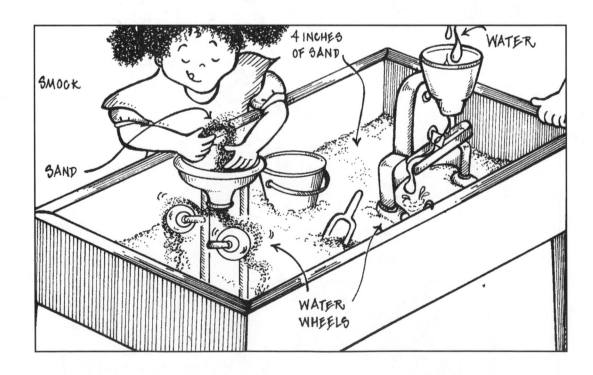

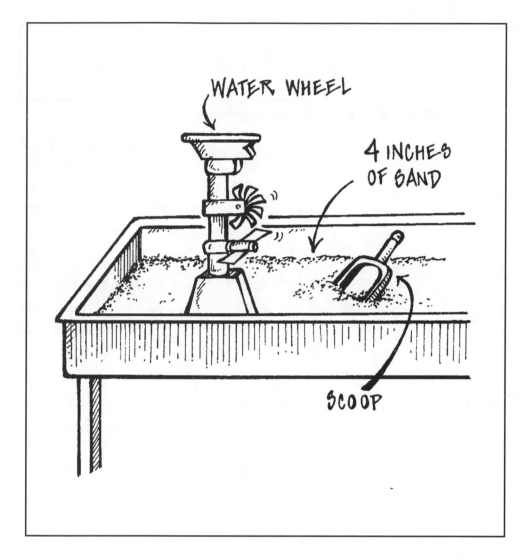

WATER WHEEL

4 INCHES OF SAND

SCOOP

Tips
Add more scoops than waterwheels to encourage the children to share.

Open-Ended Questions
How can we get the wheel to turn?

What makes the wheel turn?

Spotlight Words
Empty
Fast
Full
Slow
Turn

Legos and Water

OBJECTIVES

Emotional | Children will approach a project with expectations of success.

Intellectual | Children will work through a project and complete a task.

Social | Children will share and build on each other's ideas.

Physical | Children will increase their small motor skills.

MATERIALS

Water

Food coloring, optional

Legos

SETTING UP THE ACTIVITY

1. Put 5" (12 cm) of water in the sand and water table. Color the water, if desired.
2. Place Legos in the water. If desired, use Flexi-blocks or Duplos for variety.

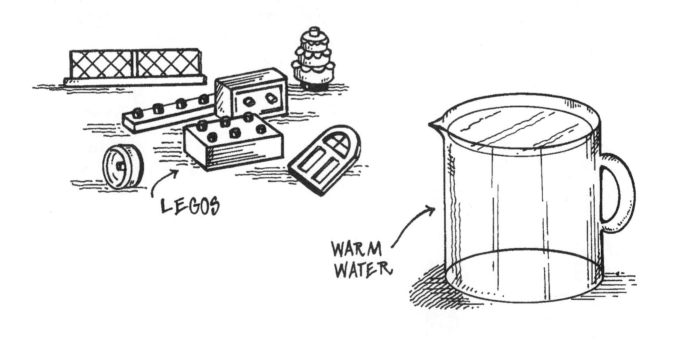

LEGOS

WARM WATER

DUPLOS

COLORED WATER

Tips

Water is an attractive medium in which to play with Legos. This activity encourages creativity and success because it is open-ended. Do not direct the children to build a boat.

Open-Ended Questions

What could we do with these Legos?

Spotlight Words

Below
Construct
Create
Design
In
On top
Out
Over
Under

Tongs and Balls

OBJECTIVES

Intellectual | *Children will practice counting skills.*
Children will discover what floats or sinks.
Social | *Children will be encouraged to cooperate*
as they work together to fill the containers.
Physical | *Children will enhance their eye-hand coordination and fine motor skills.*

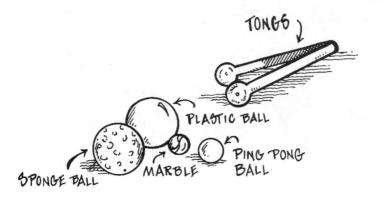

MATERIALS

Water
Food coloring, optional
Small balls (small enough to fit through
the openings of containers)
Plastic containers
Tongs (large enough to pick up the balls)

SETTING UP THE ACTIVITY

1. Fill the sand and water table half full with water. Color the water, if desired.
2. Put the small balls and plastic containers in the sand and water table.
3. Encourage the children to use tongs to pick up the balls.

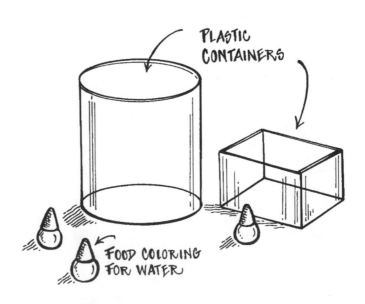

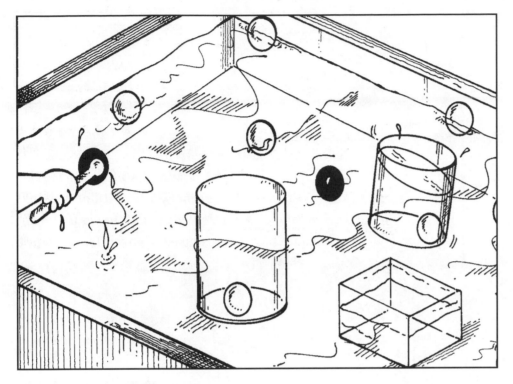

Tips

Adding a variety of balls, such as heavy large marbles, sponge balls, or wiffle golf balls, will encourage children to experiment.

Open-Ended Questions

Why do you think some things float and others sink?

How many balls will it take to fill the container?

What will happen if you drop this ball into the water?

Spotlight Words
Empty
Full
In
Out
Refill

Boats

OBJECTIVES

Intellectual | Children will learn about simple machines and how they work by building one.

Children will experiment with air as a form of energy.

Children will try out possible solutions and observe the results.

Emotional | Children will complete a project that they start.

MATERIALS

Styofoam trays or packing Styrofoam

Wooden skewers

Paper

Laminate or clear contact paper

Scissors

Glue or tape

Large rubber bands

Water

SETTING UP THE ACTIVITY

1. Help children make one of the following boats:

   Sailboat—Use Styrofoam trays or packing Styrofoam about ¼" to ½" (6 mm – 12 mm) thick for the base of the boat. Stick a wooden skewer in the center of the Styrofoam so it is balanced. Make a sail by laminating a piece of paper or covering it with clear contact paper. Cut it into a sail shape and glue or tape it to the skewer.

   Note: The taller the sail, the larger the Styrofoam base will need to be.

   Paddleboat— Use Styrofoam trays or packing Styrofoam about ¼" to ½" (6 mm – 12 mm) thick for the base of the boat. Cut out the shape of a paddleboat. Cut a smaller piece of Styrofoam to make a paddle and attach it to the boat with a wooden skewer. Place a large rubber band around the ends and twist it until it is tight, then let it go.

2. Pour water in the sand and water table.

3. Encourage the children to experiment with floating the boats in the water.

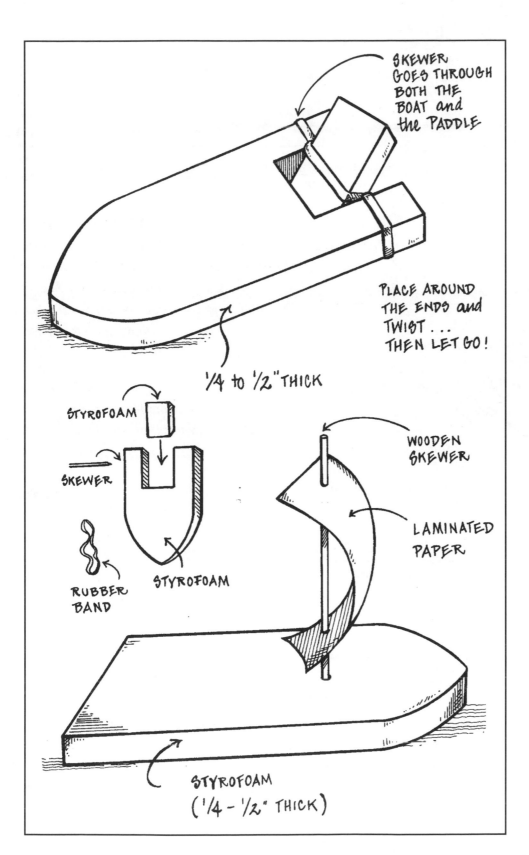

SKEWER GOES THROUGH BOTH THE BOAT and the PADDLE

PLACE AROUND THE ENDS and TWIST . . . THEN LET GO!

1/4 to 1/2" THICK

STYROFOAM

SKEWER

RUBBER BAND

STYROFOAM

WOODEN SKEWER

LAMINATED PAPER

STYROFOAM (1/4 - 1/2" THICK)

Open-Ended Questions

Why does the boat move in the water?

What could you do to make the boat move?

Did the boat move where you wanted it?

Spotlight Words

Air
Energy
Far
Fast
Near
Simple machine
Slow
Wind

Pipes and Accordion Tubing

OBJECTIVES

Intellectual | Children will experiment with building a networking system of pipes.

Social | Children will verbalize their ideas and work together towards a common goal. Children will consider the feelings of others and respect their ideas.

MATERIALS

PVC pipes, cardboard tubes, and accordion tubing (available at school supply stores and catalogs)

Tape

Marbles

Birdseed

Cups

Scoops

Tall containers

Funnels

PICK UP AND 'MOVE' MARBLE THROUGH MAZE

TAPE

SECURE CUT AREAS WITH TAPE SO THAT AREAS DO NOT SEPARATE WHEN MOVED

ANGLE CUT

SETTING UP THE ACTIVITY

1. Set up one or more of the following in the sand and water table.

   Marble Maze—Use PVC pipes or cardboard tubes, tape, and marbles.

   Water Works—Use PVC pipes or accordion tubing, tape, cups, and water.

   Grain Silo—Use birdseed, PVC pipes or accordion tubing, cups, scoops, tall containers, and funnels.

2. Try using one or more of the above with another medium (see page 11 for a list of suggestions).

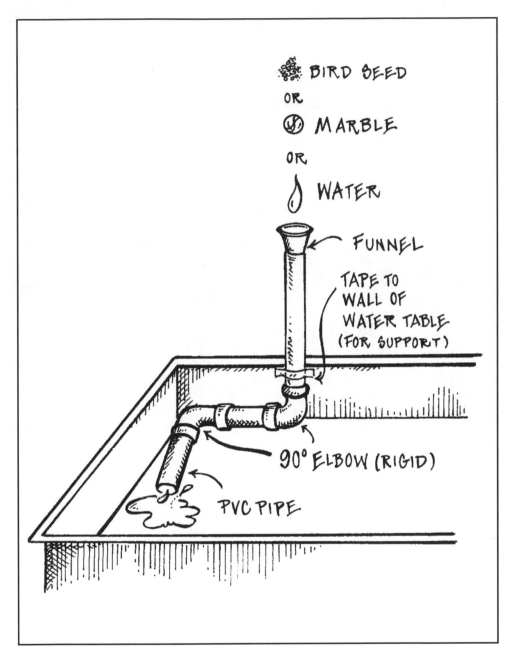

BIRD SEED
OR
MARBLE
OR
WATER

FUNNEL

TAPE TO WALL OF WATER TABLE (FOR SUPPORT)

90° ELBOW (RIGID)

PVC PIPE

Do you have any ideas?

How are you going to make those ideas work?

How do you think it will look when it is finished?

Spotlight Words

Above
Back
Below
Design
Down
Front
In
Out
Plan
System
Up

Miscellaneous Activities

Putty or Dough 104

Pumpkins 106

Wild and Wacky Word Strips 108

Crazy Counting 110

Putty or Dough

OBJECTIVES

Intellectual | *Children will compare quantities and discuss relationships, such as more, less, big, bigger, same, different, part, whole, and so on.*

Literacy | *Children will be exposed to the alphabet.*
Children will identify their own names and the names of their peers.

Emotional | *Children will have opportunities to express their hostility in positive ways.*
Children will come up with their own ideas and put those ideas into action.
Children will approach an activity with expectations of success and feel proud of themselves.

Social | *Children will respect their peers' personal space.*

Physical | *Children will practice their cutting skills.*

Diversity | *Children will talk about different skin colors in a positive way.*

MATERIALS

Tape
Recipes for Homemade Silly Putty (see page 122) or Playdough (see page 122)
Ingredients to make Homemade Silly Putty or Playdough
Scissors
Plastic figures, such as bears or dinosaurs
Popsicle sticks
Paint or food coloring
Letter mold or cookie cutters
Alphabet cards

SETTING UP THE ACTIVITY

1. If you are working on helping the children respect personal space, divide the sand and water table into six equal sections using tape.
2. In each of the six sections, place the same amount and type of materials. (For example, a handful of playdough, five plastic bears, two Popsicle sticks, and three people figures.)
3. Make Homemade Silly Putty or Playdough using the recipes on page 122.
4. Use the Silly Putty or Playdough for each of the following activities:

Cutting—Put old scissors and Playdough or Silly Putty into the sand and water table and encourage the children to practice cutting. (Save your old scissors for this activity because it may dull your new ones.)

Personal Space—Place Playdough or Silly Putty, plastic figures, and Popsicle sticks into each of the six sections of the sand and water table (see steps 1 and 2).

Creativity—Put Playdough or Silly Putty in the sand and water table and let the children's creativity take over.

Comparing—Use only Playdough. Encourage the children to compare the sizes, colors, textures, and so on of different balls of playdough.

Cause-and-effect—Make Playdough or Silly Putty with the children.

Diversity—Use paint or food coloring to color Playdough different skin colors. Encourage the children to create people sculptures and let them dry overnight.

Channel Hostility—Give Silly Putty or Playdough to a child who needs to work out her frustration.

Alphabet—Give the children letter molds or cookie cutters to use with Playdough or Silly Putty. Line the sides of the sand and water table with alphabet cards. Tape the children's names on the sides of the sand and water table. Encourage the children to find and make their own names, as well as their peers, with Playdough or Silly Putty.

Pumpkins

OBJECTIVES

Intellectual | Children will talk about yesterday, today, and tomorrow.

Children will learn the process of how a pumpkin grows.

Children will make predictions.

Literacy | Children will create their own stories.

Emotional | Children will complete the projects that they start.

Social | Children will work together in a group.

MATERIALS

Pumpkins

Knife (teacher only)

Metal spoons

Measuring cups

Water

Salt

Container

Shallow baking pan

Oven

Recipe and ingredients for making pumpkin bread, pumpkin cookies, or pumpkin pie

Books about pumpkins (see suggestions on the following page)

Paper and markers or crayons

SETTING UP THE ACTIVITY

1. Go on a field trip to a pumpkin patch to find pumpkins; plant pumpkin seeds in the spring so the children can harvest them in the fall; or purchase pumpkins.

2. Choose from the following pumpkin ideas:

   Pumpkin Seeds—Put two or three pumpkins in the sand and water table. Precut an opening in the top of the pumpkin, but do not take out the seeds. Ask the children to use metal spoons to scoop out the seeds. Encourage them to count the number of seeds inside the pumpkin. Wash and soak the seeds overnight in a container of salt water. (Use 3 cups of

water and ⅔ cup of salt.) The next day, bake the seeds in the oven at 250°
for about 3 to 4 hours, checking them periodically. Bake until the seeds are
toasted light brown. Eat the toasted seeds. Yum!

Baking—Help the children make pumpkin bread, pumpkin cookies, or
pumpkin pie using the baked pumpkin seeds.

Read—Read books about how pumpkins grow. Two suggestions are:

  It's Pumpkin Time! by Zoe Hall

  Pumpkin, Pumpkin by Jeanne Titherington

Make Books—Using paper and markers or crayons, make books with the
children about how a pumpkin grows.

Tips
Remember that learning
is a process. One activity
connects and leads to
another.

**Open-Ended
Questions**
Where do seeds come
from?

How long does it take to
grow a pumpkin?

What kind of things can
we do with the
pumpkin?

Spotlight Words
Blossoms
Harvest
Leaves
Roots
Seeds
Sprout
Stem
Today
Tomorrow
Yesterday

Wild and Wacky Word Strips

OBJECTIVES

Intellectual | Children will learn one-to-one correspondence and number recognition.

Literacy | Children will be exposed to letters and words in a meaningful and exciting way.

Emotional | Children will release tension and become absorbed in an activity.

Physical | Children will enhance small motor skills.

MATERIALS

Paper, sticky labels, or masking tape

Markers

Clear tape

Medium, such as sand, large buttons, or shredded paper (see list of suggestions on page 11)

Paintbrushes

Small objects relating to the children's interests and the objectives

SETTING UP THE ACTIVITY

1. Prepare word strips. For example, if you choose numbers, write numerals on paper, sticky labels, or masking tape and cover with clear tape. The tape will ensure that it stays in place.

2. Place the word strips on the bottom of the sand and water table.

3. Pour sand, large buttons, or shredded paper over the word strips and place paintbrushes in the sand and water table. Ask the children to use the paintbrushes to brush away the sand from the hidden word strips.

4. Encourage the children to search, identify, and match word strips with the small objects.

5. Choose the following word strip ideas, depending on the children's interests and needs. Place the word strips in the sand and water table, cover with a medium, and encourage the children to search and match the words to the objects:

Names—Write children's names on word strips. Ask the children to match them to laminated photographs of the children in the class.

Food—Laminated magazine food pictures (with the name of the food printed on the paper). Ask the children to match these with play food.

Dinosaurs—Write dinosaur names on pictures of dinosaurs and laminate them. Encourage the children to match them to dinosaur figures.

Numbers—Write numbers and the appropriate number of dots on paper. For example, draw three dots and write the number 3. Ask the children to match these with a variety of small objects.

ABC's—Write letters of the alphabet on pieces of paper. Encourage the children to match these to a matching set of letters.

Furniture names—Write the names of dollhouse furniture on pictures of dollhouse furniture. Ask the children to match these to dollhouse furniture.

Tips
The children will be motivated to participate in an activity if their interests are reflected in how the activity is set up. For example, if children are interested in dinosaurs, use dinosaur props, supplies, and books when setting up activities.

Open-Ended Questions
How many words can you find that start with the same letter?

What words do you recognize?

Spotlight Words
Alphabet
Letters
Match
Under
Words

Crazy Counting

OBJECTIVES

Intellectual | Children will learn rote counting and one-to-one correspondence. Children will practice classifying and sorting objects.

MATERIALS

Large buttons, toothpicks, paper clips, stones, plastic bears or dinosaurs, or anything else the children would like to count (see list on page 11)

SETTING UP THE ACTIVITY

1. Model how to touch the items as you count them.
2. Place different objects in the sand and water table. Ask the children to count each object by touching it and then pushing it away. This will help them to learn one-to-one correspondence.
3. Ask the children to classify the different objects in the sand and water table. Encourage the children to decide how to group the items.

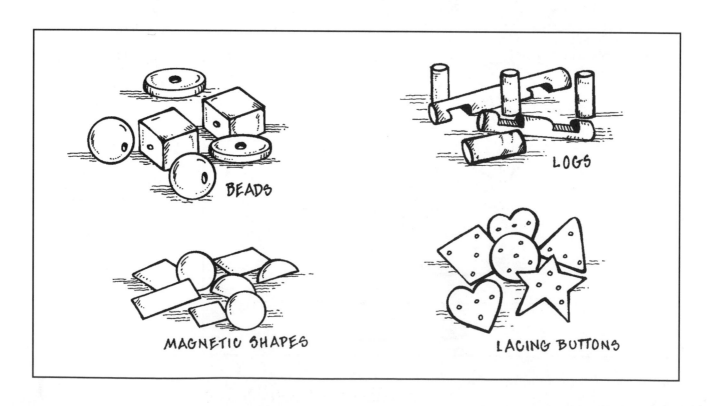

BEADS

LOGS

MAGNETIC SHAPES

LACING BUTTONS

TOOTHPICKS

LARGE BUTTONS

BEARS

MARBLES

PAPER CLIPS

Tips

If a child doesn't seem to understand the concept, don't force her. She will let you know when she is ready. Children's innate interest in the sand and water table may motivate them to count, whereas they may not be motivated with tabletop manipulatives.

Open-Ended Questions

How many are there?

What things do you think belong together?

Spotlight Words
Amount
Big
Bigger
Biggest
Count
Different
Group
Numbers
Same
Shape
Size
Total

Charts

Prediction Chart 114

Tally Sheet 115

Color Mixing 116

Signs 117

Prediction Chart

What Do You Think Will Happen?

What Happened?

Tally Sheet

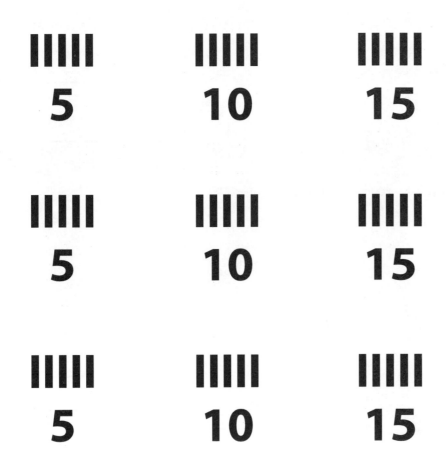

‖‖ 5	‖‖ 10	‖‖ 15
‖‖ 5	‖‖ 10	‖‖ 15
‖‖ 5	‖‖ 10	‖‖ 15

Note: The teacher should ask the children to circle the tally as the child counts or matches the amount.

Color Mixing

Blue + yellow = _____

Yellow + red = _____

Red + blue = _____

Blue + red = _____

Yellow + blue = _____

Red + yellow = _____

Note: If the children are not readers, color the words and ask the children to use crayons to record their findings.

Signs

GET WELL

HAPPY BIRTHDAY

THANK YOU

Recipes

Homemade Silly Putty 120

Playdough 120

Frilly Bubbles 121

Print Maker Bubbles 121

Hardy Bubbles 121

Brewing Bubbles 122

Oobleck 122

Salt Paint 122

Soap Paint 123

Sand Paint 123

Homemade Silly Putty

4 tablespoons (60 g) powdered starch (Faultless Starch works well)
½ cup (120 ml) water
Washable liquid paint
1 cup (240 ml) white glue

Mix together the powdered starch and water in a bowl. Stir until the starch is dissolved. Add the paint and glue to the mixture. Let it sit for a couple of minutes. Stir the mixture until it starts to set, and then knead it together with your hands. The mixture should be pliable but not sticky. Store in a zipper closure plastic bag in the refrigerator.

Note: This is a chemical reaction, so you cannot change the amounts of or substitute any of the ingredients. If the silly putty is too sticky, add more starch. Begin by adding about 1 teaspoon. It doesn't take much more to make a difference. If the putty is too stiff, it is best to start over.

Playdough

2 cups (250 g) flour
½ cup (62 g) salt
2 tablespoons (30 g) alum
Washable paint or powdered drink mix (such as Kool Aid)
⅓ cup (80 ml) vegetable oil
2 cups (480 ml) boiling water

Put the flour, salt, alum, paint or drink mix, and oil in a bowl. Pour boiling water over the ingredients and mix. Knead with your hands until it is the desired consistency. If it is too sticky, add more flour. Store in a zipper closure plastic bag or covered container in the refrigerator.

Frilly Bubbles

1 cup (240 ml) water
$\frac{1}{4}$ cup (30 g) sugar
$\frac{1}{2}$ cup (120 ml) liquid detergent (Joy seems to work best)
1 tablespoon (15 ml) glycerin

Mix together all of the ingredients until the sugar dissolves. Then, let the mixture stand for 3 to 4 hours.

Print Maker Bubbles

2 cups (480 ml) washable paint
1 cup (240) water
$\frac{1}{2}$ cup (120 ml) liquid starch
1 cup (240 ml) liquid detergent

Mix together all the ingredients in a bowl.

Hardy Bubbles

Water
$\frac{2}{3}$ cup (160 ml) liquid detergent (Dawn seems to work best)
1 tablespoon (15 ml) glycerin

Add enough water to the liquid detergent to make a gallon of liquid. Add the glycerin. Let the mixture sit for one day. Stir before using.

Brewing Bubbles

2 cups (480 ml) liquid detergent (Joy seems to work best)
6 cups (1440 ml) water
¾ cup (95 g) sugar

Mix together all of the ingredients. Let the mixture stand for 4 hours at room temperature.

Oobleck

2 parts cornstarch
1 part water
Washable liquid paint

Mix the water with the cornstarch. The mixture should look like a solid, but when you grab a handful, it will become runny and drip out of your hand. If the mixture is too runny and will not form a solid ball, add more cornstarch. If it is too hard, add a little more water (begin with ¼ cup). You can make as much or as little oobleck as you need—just use the right proportions. Add drops of different colors of washable paint.

Salt Paint

⅔ cup (85 g) salt
½ teaspoon (2 ml) washable liquid paint
Pinch of talcum powder or cornstarch

Mix the ingredients together thoroughly. Spread the mixture on a cookie sheet or a flat metal or plastic tray to dry. When it is dry, pour it into a large-hole salt-shaker.

Soap Paint

3 cups (270 g) soap flakes
1 ½ cups (360 ml) hot water

Pour the soap flakes and water in a plastic mixing bowl or ice cream bucket. Whip the mixture with an eggbeater until it is stiff. Do not attempt to store; mix and use the paint as needed.
Note: This paint is nice to use on dark blue paper to create a snow scene.

Sand Paint

1 cup (125 g) sifted, clean, dry sand
2 tablespoons (30 g) powdered tempera
Watered down glue

Mix together the sand and tempera thoroughly. Draw a sketch of a picture on paper or poster board. Then, brush watered glue on the sketch where you want to put the sand. Shake the sand paint onto the brushed surface.
Note: Empty talcum powder containers with shaker tops or saltshakers with large-hole shaker tops make good sand paint containers.

Index

A

Accordion tubing, 100
Airplanes, 44
Alphabet (*See also* Letters)
    cards, 104
    charts, 18
Alum, 120
Animal figures, 11
    arctic, 42
    desert, 48
    farm, 48
    jungle, 48
    ocean, 48
    pond, 48
    ranch, 48
    savannah, 48
    zoo, 48
Animal
    homes, 48–49
Aprons, 26
Aquarium rocks, 11, 46, 48
Arctic animal figures, 42
Astronaut figures, 38

B

Baby clothes, 28
Baby powder containers, 28
Baking activities, 106
Baking pans, 106
Baking soda, 80
Balance scales, 11, 28
Balls, 11, 14, 97
    beach, 52
    cotton, 68
    golf, 14, 97
    magnetic, 14, 71
    Ping-Pong, 11, 14, 68, 97
    plastic, 14, 97
    sponge, 97
    whiffle, 97
Barns, 48
Baskets, 20
Bathing materials, 28
Beach balls, 52

Beach towels, 52
Beach umbrellas, 52
Beads/lacing, 11
Bear figures, 104, 110
Berry baskets, 20
Birdseed, 11, 100
Birthday candles, 76
Blocks, 71
Board books, 28
Boats, 11, 40, 52, 96
    homemade, 98–99
Bolts, 11, 74
Books
    about pumpkins, 106
    Bartholomew and the Oobleck by Dr.
        Seuss, 79
    board, 28
    homemade, 56, 107
    It's Pumpkin Time! by Zoe Hall, 107
    Pumpkins, Pumpkins by Jeanne
        Titherington, 107
    A Rainbow of My Own by Don
        Freeman, 64
Bottles
    baby lotion, 28
    shampoo, 28
    spray, 60
    squirt, 82
Bowls, 11, 48, 78
    mixing, 26, 120–123
    plastic, 86
Bread, 106–107
Brewing bubbles, 121
Bubble mixes, 11, 20, 62
    brewing, 122
    frilly, 121
    hardy, 121
    print maker, 121
    recipes, 121–122
Bubble wands, 20, 62
Buckets, 11, 54, 60
    ice cream, 82
Bulldozers, 36
Butcher paper, 14, 16, 22
Buttons, 11, 42, 71, 108, 110

C

Cacti
    plastic, 48
Cameras, 55
Candles, 76
Candy molds, 82
Cardboard, 72
    corrugated, 72
    packing corners, 46
    tubes, 100
Cards, 26
    alphabet, 104
    index, 84
    tally, 90, 115
Cars, 11, 44, 71
Cash registers, 30
Cassette recorders, 28, 49, 62
Chalk, 16
Charts, 113–117
    color mixing, 116
    prediction, 78, 80, 82, 86, 114
    signs, 117–118
    tally sheets, 90, 115
Chocolate bars, 76
Clay pots, 30
Clipboards, 86
Coat hangers, 20
Coffee filters, 86
Coins, 72
Color mixing chart, 116
Construction paper, 14, 16, 20, 72
Contact paper
    clear, 98
Containers, 14, 46, 78, 106
    clear plastic, 80, 90
    large, 80
    margarine, 78
    plastic, 96
    small, 42, 64
    tall, 11, 20, 100
Cookie cutters, 11, 26, 104
Cookies, 106–107
Cooking equipment, 26

Coral, 40
Cork, 40, 48
Cornstarch, 78, 122
Cotton balls, 68
Cottonseed, 11
Crayons, 32, 72, 76, 106
    shavings, 22
Cupcake pans, 26
Cups, 48, 100
    clear plastic, 80, 85
    measuring, 11, 78, 80, 90, 106,
        120–123
    Styrofoam, 74

D
Dandelions, 56
Dawn dishwashing liquid, 28, 90, 121
Desert animal figures, 48
Diapers, 28
Dinosaurs
    figures, 11, 32, 46, 104, 109–110
    pictures, 109
Dirt, 58
Dishcloths, 60
Dishwashing liquid, 28, 90, 121–122
Diversity objectives
    defined, 10
    dramatic play activities, 26–29, 32–33
    environment activities, 36–37, 46–49
    miscellaneous activity, 104
    science activity, 86–87
Dollhouse furniture, 109
Dolls, 11
    multicultural, 28
Drink mix, 120
Duplos, 94

E
Easter grass, 11
Egg beaters, 11
Eggs
    plastic, 11, 46
Elephant figures, 48
Emotional objectives
    art activities, 14–19, 22–23
    defined, 9
    dramatic play activities, 26–29, 32–33
    environment activities, 38–43, 46–49
    miscellaneous activities, 104–109
    outdoor activities, 52–57, 62–63
    science activities, 68–69, 72–73,
        78–80, 82–83
    water activities, 90–91, 94–95, 98–99
Eyedroppers, 11, 42, 86, 90
Eye-hand coordination builders, 14, 54,
    86, 90, 96

F
Fabric strips, 42
Farm animal figures, 48
Faultless Starch, 120
Feathers, 68
Film, 55
Fine motor skill builders, 16, 22, 32, 42,
    86, 94, 104, 108
Fingerpaints, 11, 16
Fish figures, 40
Flexi-Blocks, 94
Flour sifters, 11, 26
Flour, 120
Flower pots, 30
Flowers, 22, 82
    plastic, 30, 58
    silk, 30
Foil, 76
Food coloring, 42, 48, 78, 82, 84, 94, 96,
    104
Foods, 106–107
    caution, 10
Freezers, 42
Frilly bubbles, 121
Frog figures, 48
Funnels, 11, 90, 100

G
Garden hoses, 64
Gardening tools, 58
Garlic presses, 11
Gelatin, 78
Giraffe figures, 48
Glasses
    clear plastic, 84
Gloves, 42
Glue, 36, 72, 98, 120
    sticks, 73
    watered down, 22, 123
Glycerin, 121
Golf balls, 14
    whiffle, 97
Grass, 56
    clippings, 48
    Easter, 11

H
Hard hats, 36
Hardy bubbles, 62
    recipe, 121
Hats
    construction worker, 36
    sun, 52
Hoes, 58
Hole punches, 72
Horse figures, 48
Hula hoops, 62

I
Ice cream buckets, 82
Ice cube trays, 42, 82
Ice cubes, 11, 76, 78
Index cards, 84
Insect figures, 11
Intellectual objectives
    art activities, 14–19
    defined, 9
    dramatic play activities, 30–33
    environment activities, 38–39, 46–49
    miscellaneous activities, 104–111
    outdoor activities, 54–65
    science activities, 68–87
    water activities, 90–101
Irons, 22

J
Jars, 77
Jell-O molds, 82
Joy dishwashing liquid, 28, 90, 121–122
Jungle animal figures, 48

K
Kitchen utensils, 20, 26
Knives, 106
    plastic, 32, 82
Kool Aid, 120

L
Lab coats, 86
Laminate, 98, 109
Large motor skills, 60, 62
Leaves, 11, 22, 56, 68, 72
Legos, 11, 48, 72, 94
Letters, 109
    molds, 82, 104
    plastic, 11
Lincoln Logs, 48
Lion figures, 48
Liquid starch, 16, 121
Liquid Watercolors, 90
Literacy objectives
    art activity, 18–19
    defined, 9
    dramatic play activities, 26–27, 30–33
    environment activities, 36–37, 40–41,
        44–49
    miscellaneous activities, 104–109
    outdoor activities, 56–57, 60–61,
        64–65
    science activities, 72–77, 80–83,
        86–87
Lizard figures, 48
Lotion bottles, 28

M

Magazine pictures, 109
Magnetic balls, 14, 71
Magnets, 70
Magnifying glasses, 11
Marble tunnels, 11
Marbles, 11, 97, 100
    magnetic, 14, 71
Margarine containers, 78
Markers, 30, 32, 36, 60, 68, 72, 106, 108
Masking tape, 68, 108
Measuring cups, 11, 78, 80, 90, 106, 120–123
Measuring spoons, 11, 16, 90, 120–123
Melon scoops, 11
Melting objects, 76
Metal objects, 70, 74
    spoons, 106
Mirrors, 64
Mixing spoons, 26
Molds, 82
    letters, 82, 104
    sand, 42, 54, 82
Moon vehicles, 38
Mud, 11
Muffin tins, 11, 27
Music
    lullabies, 28
    soothing, 62

N

Numbers, 109
    plastic, 11
Nuts (metal), 11, 74

O

Ocean animal figures, 48, 52
Oobleck, 11, 78–79
    recipe, 122
Open-ended questions, 15
Ovens, 106

P

Packing materials, 11, 46, 68, 98
Paintbrushes, 108
Paints, 104
    liquid washable, 18, 20, 78, 86, 90, 120–122
    recipes, 122–123
    salt, 122–123
    sand, 123
    soap, 123
    tempera, 14, 16, 123
Paper clips, 74, 110

Paper towels, 84
Paper, 11, 26, 32, 56, 98, 106, 108
    butcher, 14, 16, 22
    construction, 14, 16, 20, 72
    contact, 98
    shredded, 11, 48, 108
    tissue, 22, 68
Parsley, 83
Pasta, 10
Paste, 72
Pebbles, 32
Pencils, 86
Penguin figures, 42
Pens, 26, 30, 56
People figures, 11, 40, 42, 44, 48, 52, 64
    astronauts, 38
Physical objectives
    art activities, 14–17, 22–23
    defined, 10
    environment activities, 32–33, 42–43
    eye-hand coordination, 14, 54, 86, 90, 96
    fine motor skills, 16, 22, 32, 42, 86, 94, 104, 108
    large motor skills, 60, 62
    miscellaneous activities, 104–105, 108–109
    outdoor activities, 54–55, 60–63
    science activity, 86–87
    water activities, 90–91, 94–97
Pie tins, 20
Pies, 106–107
Ping-Pong balls, 11, 14, 68, 97
Pipe cleaners, 20
Plant flats, 30
Plants, 82
    plastic, 11, 30, 46, 48, 58
    silk, 30
Plaster of Paris, 32
Plastic figures
    animals, 11
    arctic animals, 42
    astronauts, 38
    bears, 104, 110
    desert animals, 48
    dinosaurs, 11, 32, 46, 104, 109–110
    farm animals, 48
    fish, 40
    jungle animals, 48
    ocean animals, 48, 52
    people, 11, 40, 42, 44, 48, 52, 64
    ranch animals, 48
    savannah animals, 48
    zoo animals, 48

Plastic objects, 70
    balls, 14, 97
    bowls, 86
    eggs, 11, 46
    pots, 30
    six-pack rings, 20
    syringes, 84, 90
    tablecloths, 46
    test tubes, 86
    trays, 72
    tubing, 20, 84, 90
Plates, 72
Play money, 30, 60
Playdough, 11, 26
    homemade, 104
    recipe, 120
Polar bear figures, 42
Ponds, 48
Popcorn molds, 82
Popsicle sticks, 30, 32, 36, 42, 82, 104
Poster board, 36, 60
Pots
    clay, 30
    plastic, 30
Potting soil, 11, 30, 58
Powdered drink mix, 120
Powdered starch, 120
Prediction charts, 78, 80, 82, 86
    sample, 114
Print makers bubbles, 121
Pumpkins, 106
Puzzle pieces, 71
PVC pipes, 100

Q ~ R

Rags, 60
Rakes, 58
Ranch animal figures, 48
Recipes, 26, 119–123
    brewing bubbles, 122
    class book of, 56
    frilly bubbles, 121
    from home, 27
    hardy bubbles, 121
    imaginary, 27
    oobleck, 122
    playdough, 120
    print maker bubbles, 121
    pumpkin, 106
    salt paint, 122–123
    sand paint, 123
    silly putty, 120
    soap paint, 123
Rock salt, 11, 38, 82

Rocking chairs, 28
Rocks, 32, 36, 38, 44, 56, 68, 82, 110
    aquarium, 11, 46, 48
    colored, 48
Rolling pins, 26
Rubber bands, 98

S

Salt, 106, 120, 122
Salt paint, 122–123
Saltshakers, 16
Sand, 11, 32, 36, 44, 48, 52, 54, 56, 58, 70,
    92, 108, 123
Sand molds, 42, 54, 82
Sand paint, 123
Savannah animal figures, 48
Sawdust, 11, 48
Scissors, 11, 22, 98, 104
Scoops, 11, 92, 100
Scrapbooks, 55
Screws, 71
Scrubbers, 60
Seal figures, 42
Seeds, 58
    pumpkin, 106
Shampoo bottles, 28
Shapes, 11
Shaving cream, 11, 18
    caution, 19
Shells, 32, 40, 48, 52, 72
Shirts
    adult-size, 86
Shovels, 11, 30, 42, 54, 58
Signs
    car wash, 60–61
    do not touch, 55
    patterns, 117–118
    traffic, 37, 118
Silly putty, 11
    homemade, 104
    recipe, 120
Smocks, 14, 16, 18, 56
Snacks, 106–107
Snake figures, 48
Snow, 11, 42, 76
Soap, 60
    bar, 28
    dishwashing, 28, 90
    flakes, 123
Soap paint, 123
Social objectives
    defined, 10
    dramatic play activities, 26–31
    environment activities, 36–49

miscellaneous activities, 104–107
outdoor activities, 52–61, 64–65
science activities, 70–87
water activities, 90–97, 100–101
Soybeans, 11
Space shuttles, 38
Spinning tops, 11
Sponge balls, 97
Sponges, 11, 28
Spoons, 78
    measuring, 11, 16, 90, 120–123
    metal, 106
    mixing, 26
Spotlight words, 15
Spray bottles, 60
Sprinklers, 64
Squirt bottles, 82
Starch
    liquid, 16, 121
    powdered, 120
Stencils, 73
Sticks, 56
Sticky labels, 30, 108
Strainers, 11
Straw, 48
Straws, 11, 20, 68
String, 72
Styrofoam, 40, 48, 68, 74
    cups, 74
    packing peanuts, 98
    trays, 98
Sugar, 121–122
Sun hats, 52
Sunglasses, 52
Syringes, 84, 90

T

Tablecloths, 46
Talcum powder, 122
Tally cards, 90
    pattern, 115
Tape, 98, 100, 108
    masking, 68, 108
Tempera paints, 14
    powdered, 16, 123
Test tubes, 11, 86
Textured items, 72
Tissue paper, 22, 68
Tongs, 11, 96
Toothpicks, 110
Towels, 28, 60
    beach, 52
    paper, 84
Trays

plastic, 72
Styrofoam, 98
Tricycles, 60
Trucks, 11, 36, 44, 48
Tubing
    accordion, 100
    cardboard, 100
Tubing, 20, 84, 90

U

Umbrellas
    beach, 52

V

Vegetable oil, 120
Videotape recorder, 62
Videotape, 62
Vinegar, 80

W

Walrus figures, 42
Warming trays, 76
Washcloths, 28
Water, 11, 14, 28, 40, 46, 48, 52, 54, 60, 74,
    78, 82, 84, 86, 90–101, 106, 120–123
Water mills, 11
Watering cans, 30, 56, 58
Waterwheels, 92
Waxed paper, 22
Whiffle balls, 97
Whisks, 11
Wood, 74
    objects, 70
    skewers, 98
    strips, 108–109
Worms, 11

Z

Zebra figures, 48
Zoo animal figures, 48